ON THE ROAD TO MANHOOD

A Manual for Men

"Transitioning out of dark places to cross the divide separating boys from men"

Martin E. Thomas

ACKNOWLEDGEMENT

I made a list of the people who have been directly involved with me over the past few months. I was interested in identifying those without whom the challenges I faced transitioning from the "outer world" I'd inhabited for the past 21 years would have been nearly insurmountable. The list only served to complicate my efforts to isolate the people I needed to acknowledge in this book. For every one person I wanted to mention, there are others whose contributions to my life are vital. Therefore, it is simply impossible to mention specifically those dear friends whose love and support carried me during one of the most delicate periods of my adult life. Actually, I will never be able to adequately thank them in any format.

Accordingly, I want to acknowledge that there is small tribe of blessed souls, men and women, who have invested themselves in doing all that was necessary, making whatever sacrifice the moment demanded of them to insure that I found my way back to some semblance of normality in the world. They know who they are and will accept this general attempt on my part to say thank you as a group for loving me unconditionally.

I call her "Carolyn Jean." The fact that she is my life partner and wife might seem to some reason enough to mention her by name. Still, as significant as those aspects of our relationship are, Carolyn's role in my life is more than that and cannot be overstated. Among the many things she has done over the past five years to ready a path for me to continue my life's journey with a high level of dignity, one thing directly related to the completion of this book is noteworthy. Carolyn Jean believes in me. It is the highest honor bestowed on me by a woman in my entire life. Of course, her love for me knows no barrier. Oh my goodness, how she loves me! In the strength of that love, Carolyn Jean demonstrates daily that there is nothing within her ability or power that can hinder the extent to which she will give of herself to advance that to which I have committed my life. In this way, she has made her life mine. But it is the impact that her faith in me has; and her indescribable ability to push me toward reaching with excellence my goals to achieve my full potential that I acknowledge her. So, to the one who has convinced me that I am able to jump a ten-foot wall, Carolyn Jean, thank you.

DEDICATION

This book is dedicated to my brothers at Indiana State Prison. You accepted me without expectations. I entered a prison environment as prepared to face the challenges of my new existence like a fish violently pulled out of water attached to a hook, string and pole. You watched out for me and helped until I could get my feet moving on solid ground; and even then you never left me alone. By the grace of God, I made it, largely because of your friendship. You are forever my brothers, my friends, my angels. May you find peace at every stage of your journey.

Not to disregard the women in my family circle whose place in my life and heart has defined, and at times redefined who I am, I want to also dedicate this book to my five Sons, Martin, Maurice, Marcus, Marvin, Marlon and my grandsons.

You are the reason my ancestors ever existed, the spark that gives vitality to my life. All that I am and do in this world is in the hopes that you will be whole, well, purposeful, productive and prosperous. According to the Divine order, at my journey's end, you will remain and be the only reason I was ever alive. May your journeys lead you safely across the male divide from boys to men, empowering you to take your rightful place.

My prayer is that you will find information in these pages to enlighten and inspire you to strive with all your being and courage to be God's man in your parts of the world.

CONTENTS

Copyright

Ordering information

Quantity Sales. Special discounts are available for bulk purchases by corporations, associations, networking groups. For details contact
met@fsfg.org
www.fsfg.org

Individual Sales- Contact Martin E. Thomas

Preface

So what gives me the right to address this subject and attempt to open yet another discussion on male issues? I've known for a long time that I was going to write this book. To tell the truth, I have started lettering many times but was unable to complete it due to being dissatisfied with the person I had become. Therefore, I was never able to get past this question, which haunted me like the dread of having to face a sentencing judge. If you have ever seen a trial, you may know that by the sentencing phase of a case the defendant pretty much knows the outcome. The prosecutor has suggested a certain end result, which seems consistent with the juror's body language and how rapidly they reached the guilty conviction. The sentence investigator's report in most cases recommends the same course of action prescribed by the prosecutor and the media has forecasted the "will of the public." Still, there is nothing like the wrenching feeling in your gut when the judge speaks, followed by the piercing sound of the gavel that affirms his action and seals your fate.

The anxiety I felt dealing with this question was like that. It concerns the issue of credibility. This seemed a problem for me considering my present circumstances, not to mention the highs and lows of an eventful past. Every writer should know that integrity is an essential part of being able to attract the attention of one's intended audience. Earning the right to speak on a subject requires one to demonstrate that he or she has the standing or authority to address the area under discussion. If he fails, this litmus test his words will likely fall on deaf ears. Clearly, if I were unable (or unwilling, as was really the case) to write honestly about myself, even to the point of discomfort on some matters, then it was possible that I could never gain an acceptable level of credibility with some people. What's more, the goal of this book could not be achieved. So, even if I succeeded to get a few copies of the finished book off the shelf, if I could not establish credibility, then the work would still be a failure. No doubt you would agree that if one knows in advance a particular project is doomed to failure, it is unwise to proceed with the venture until the hindrance is removed. But I really wanted to write a book that would be a helpful guide for turning a bad situation into a good one. I imagined that the project would inspire hope and give direction to men and women who have lost their way and are incarcerated (or moving in that direction), literally hundreds and thousands of people in jails and prisons across this land. Also I wanted the material to offer practical insights for caretakers looking for effective ways to reach this demographic of the population.

I wanted to share the insights gained during my own incarceration. The valuable and useful understandings I gleaned from a variety of individual counseling sessions and encounters, group discussions, and extraordinary life situations that open a new awareness into the mindsets of offenders, particularly hardened, career criminals. My hope was that this would offer a rare and helpful perspective for students and providers of prison systems. So, given these aspirations, there was no way around this imposing question, "What gives me the right to address this subject?" Which also meant I could not avoid the possible negative impact that telling my stories might have on those whose lives intersected mine at various points here and there.

On the other hand, if I wanted this undertaking to be more than just another book about some guy "doing time," or if it was to be taken seriously and actually used to guide others, then I would have to expose things about myself that were not very pleasant. That realization gave me pause. Why? Because depending on where this self-exposure led me, revealing my secrets could adversely affect the few small parts of my reputation that survived my own incarceration, possibly alienate the very people I wanted to reach, and it would definitely force me to face a painful reality—I had not been a very credible person for an incredibly long period of my life, and I was not looking forward to openly saying so if it was not absolutely necessary.

My first attempt at establishing credibility to write on this subject was to admit that I have for many years floated untrue information about myself. Indeed, my oldest, most familiar, and most difficult personal struggle has been lying to impress others, or attempting to add power to my words (or so I thought). Sadly, I habitually misrepresented facts, left out important details, and/or altered information on matters and issues for no good reason at all. This mindset is common among incarcerated people and I knew it was important for me to confess that really at the core, "I was one of them."

The very fact that I had been incarcerated might appear to some observers to make this point obvious. But I have enjoyed the highest level of respect possible from prison residents and Corrections staff members from the day I was arrested in 1996. Everyone knew that I had been a respected pastor in Kansas City, and my behavior and words from the beginning of incarceration and throughout the years remained consistent with how people generally regard those "called by God." So I was always considered "different from everybody else" and received a degree of difference treatment. Even the sentencing Judge in my case had called me "an anomaly unlike any who had come before him in the 26 years he had been on the bench." It was true; I was different from many other "offenders" in the system. I cannot tell you how many times through the years of incarceration I was told that I "did not belong in prison." And I was treated differently. Many officers actually apologized when they had to do routine cell inspections (shake downs) and my property was never tossed around like so many others. There were times when I would request the officer in charge of my housing unit to shake down my property and treat me like everyone else.

However, despite the respect I received by others, I knew that I was not the authentic person inside that I projected so well outside. The "risk-free" lies I'd uttered about myself, for many years, became so commonplace that at times I would have to think about what was and was not the truth of a given matter. As a way of soothing a faulty conscience, I dismissed these lies as "little white tales." And since my tales were about things of no real consequence to anyone, was mostly unpopular information about subject, not many knew or cared about and that on reflection now, neither improved my standing at the time nor diminished others in any way, I reasoned that my slippery tongue was not so bad. Besides, everyone has some faults, right?

I now know that these lies damaged me in immeasurable ways and blocked every opportunity I have had to reach my fullest potential. To my utter disappointment I see clearly that my tales have affected every relationship I have had throughout my entire life, including how I relate with God, family and myself. When I pledged never to lie again, about anything, to any one, for any reason, I spent countless hours trying to understand why I had ever lied so much in the first place. Why had I developed the habit of stretching the truth? How had I permitted myself to get to the point where I would lie about ordinary things that did not matter at all? I answer those questions and deal with this whole issue more fully below. But one example will explain how harmful lying can really be; or at least, how hurtful it was to me.

I remember visiting Jacksonville, Florida on my first major trip away from home alone in 1973. I had just turned 17 years old and it surprised me that my parents so easily agreed to the trip. But I was due to graduate from High School in a few weeks, and apparently they felt it was time for me to be emancipated. The two-week vacation was to be spent with a Christian family in a proper environment. I had met some of the young people I would see in Jacksonville the previous summer, while attending a Youth Conference in Winter Park, Florida. They all seemed of decent character. Plus, my parents were aware that I was determined to move away from home on the very day I completed High School and Florida was one of the places I wanted to visit as a prospective new home. I arrived in the middle of the week and the vacation was going great, until we went to church on Sunday morning.

The congregation's youth group was much larger than my home church back in Pontiac, Michigan. They were impressive too. Listening to some of them speak about their lives, plans and goals, I soon realized that they were so much further advanced than me. Some of the teenagers thought my proper accent and "northern ways" were a little strange. It's easy for me to see now that I felt inferior to them and wanted very much to be accepted. So to compensate for the inadequacies I felt, I told lies about myself that helped me appear more sophisticated and mature. Regrettably, little did I know at the time that my lies would have the lasting effect of helping to shape my life. I spent years trying unsuccessfully to live up to the high standards my lies set for me.

Saying that I was a young preacher was among the lies I told the young people about myself. My girlfriend's mother, in whose home I was staying, proudly repeated the story to the pastor. When he asked me, I added to the lie, enjoying the attention and related my plans to become a pastor myself one day. That was a huge lie. It was true that I had given several speeches at youth rallies and events sponsored by our denomination. I had even won a number of significant church awards and trophies. Since being in Junior High School, I participated in numerous local and state speech contests, receiving my share of recognition and trophies. But I was no preacher. And I definitely had no thought of ever being a pastor. In fact, at that point in my life, I had made no plans for the future whatsoever, even though I was a few months away from graduating High School.

Anyway, the pastor introduced me to the congregation that morning and surprised them, and me, with the announcement that on the following Sunday I would be the guest speaker. Instantly I was received and accepted by my peers and everyone else as one worthy of special respect.

Of course, I was experienced with preparing a speech. And even though I had never given a sermon, Lord knows I heard enough sermons, having been "raised in the church." I spent the entire week of my vacation preparing to present myself as a true "man of God" would, hoping not to be embarrassed or discovered as an impostor.

The sermon focused on the occasion of Jesus' first trial when one of his chief followers, Peter, lied about knowing him. I remember struggling with whether I should confess my own lies then and there. I wanted too, but how would it be received? It was too risky, so instead I played the role superbly, called forth the years of training in the art of speech giving, gave an acceptable performance, and afterwards enjoyed the accolades of the pastor and members, especially the young people, whose respect I craved.

A few months later I moved to Florida to be around those young people and attend church. It had not occurred to me that everyone would greet and respect me as a young preacher or that they would expect me to live up to that role. And I was left speechless each time the pastor insisted I take on responsibilities consistent with a young minister. He required me to represent him and the church at denominational functions. Soon I was preaching at the church in a regular rotation and often filling in for the pastor when he was unable to preach. There I was having received no higher calling from God, with not even a shallow desire to be a preacher.

I struggled on several occasions to expose my dilemma to the pastor, to tell the truth and to solicit his help to get myself out of this awful jam, but the opportunity to confess was never quite right. Many times when I would attempt to downgrade myself and reveal my inner turmoil, he would commend my dutiful service and obedience to his authority and piled more responsibility on me. And the more he pressed, the harder I strove to excel and not disappoint him. Soon I was receiving recognition from other pastors and invitations to preach, to make remarks at a special gathering, or to work on some committee dealing with youth issues. It wasn't long before I settled into the ideal of being a preacher, since I had no other plans for my life.

The big problem for me was that I was not worthy. I was spiritually and morally immature. There were things I wanted to do and places I wanted to visit. I wanted to experiment with life, be out on my own, live as I pleased and find my way in the world like the other young people. But I couldn't, because I was a "man of God." Adults depended on me to set a proper example for other young people to follow. I was stuck. My life was miserable with the way I belonged to everyone else and how public my life had become. If I did anything that was considered "worldly," I had to conceal it from everyone to avoid offense. But nothing I did was ever good enough, or so I thought. In time I was constantly questioning my motives, examining my deeds, striving to remove imperfections that revealed that I was not the man everyone thought. Soon I learned to be alone, to keep secrets, and worst of all to lie.

When I wanted to enjoy some entertainment function like the other young people my age, to go to a theater or attend a concert, I would drive on the other side of town or to a nearby city; because I could not be certain if my "fun time" would offend someone. And even though, personally, I did not agree with the old pastor's teaching that going to the theater or a concert was a great sin, when asked about the issue I spoke publically about the evils of the "big-screen," warning against sex, violence and greed. Around people I was serious, prayerful, and focused on heaven. I even trained myself not to laugh at a funny joke if it was about an unseemly subject or the person used a few "choice words." Any fun I enjoyed had to be done alone, or among strangers, but always out of the watchful eye of the church.

Perhaps, I should mention at this point that my parents had raised me to be a disciplined person and to take the Christian lifestyle seriously. And I did. Although, I had not made plans to become a pastor, I did want to be a Christian and was determined to live a life worthy of that call. However, the folly of youth was as strong in my mind as it was with many other young people. I was 17 years old and I wanted to have a little fun like all the other kids my age. But I couldn't because I was "the young preacher." Parents looked up to me and solicited my help with their children. Some even wanted their sons to follow my example and their daughters to marry a guy like me.

I was okay with the attention and always proud of my values and the discipline instilled in me by a godly mother and very demanding father. I fostered no desire to be "buck wild" or to do really bad things that would lead to an ungodly lifestyle. But increasingly I was becoming a lonely person, living with a gnawing shame that I was operating my life under false pretenses and being recognized by everyone as a "holy man." No matter how hard I worked to rid myself of this dreadful feeling it never subsided.

Eventually I attended a Christian college in Texas that was prominent in our denomination for training preachers. In time I was invited to work with a church in Mineral Wells, Texas, and soon thereafter was called to be a minister at a prominent church in Kansas City, Missouri. Through the years I have been a member of several important boards, worked in very influential circles and have preached to audiences large and small around the globe. As the years past, I became one of the most respected and sought after young preachers in our denomination. Before leaving Florida, I married a church girl with a singular pressing ambition to love and marry a godly man, raise a godly family, work in the church and live happily ever after. We set out to fulfill her desires, raised five sons, and conducted a largely successful ministry together for over 20 years. But my whole life was partially based on that one false statement I told on a Sunday morning in Florida in 1973. Have I been sincere in my life's work? Very! Has God used me to carry out deeds for him? Most definitely! Has the Lord been in my life and worked through me all these years to be a blessing to others? Certainly! Still, I lied and the strength of that one false statement has guided my entire life.

This is not the first time I have told that story, but it is an example of the type of lies I have told about myself and the long lasting consequences that ensued. I have exaggerated in sermons, embellished stories in classes, stretched facts in counseling sessions, and misrepresented myself in casual conversations for many years. In fact, lying to the police about what happened on the day I was arrested and continuing to perpetuate it, while refusing to tell the truth, is partly responsible for why I was eventually convicted, sentenced and incarcerated in the manner I was. Interestingly, I was able to immediately explain my situation to the men I met in prison. But sadly, 10 years passed before I was willing to confess to my family the lie I told them and authorities the day I was arrested. Even then I wrote the story and distributed copies throughout the family due to the shame of facing them in person with the issue.

Several of my sons reacted intensely to the revelation. They did not appreciate having been lied to and were settled with the fact that the nightmare of their lives was entirely due to evil men and circumstances beyond my control, as they had been told. It was not welcomed news that their father had taken a man's life, regardless of the fact that it was apparently to protect himself and his family. They will not be happy to know that I have lied about many things in my life. However, this book was written for them also. And it was written for the people I hope to reach most; for people at risk and incarcerated people at the bottom rung of life's ladder; for those who never had the chances I or even my sons had at a normal life.

So why is this book important? Everyone has a story. I knew that I did not intend to put any lies about myself into print. I had the strong belief that being open about the things I did, about my failures, my struggles, the demons I faced could perhaps persuade others to confront their challenges with the courage it takes to defeat and overcome the

17

difficult internal conflicts that hinder personal growth. Furthermore, it is possible that there are others having similar identity issues I faced as a young man. Not related to ministry, but people who are fulfilling the goals and dreams of others and do not know how to find a safe path to travel, while they discover who they are and what they want to be in life. And still others who are already trapped by the bad decisions and consequences of lifestyles that were misdirected and are looking for a way out of the mess they have made of their lives.

On the Road to Manhood, must address these and other issues if it is to achieve the purposes for which it was undertaken. Otherwise, this book will be just another book. On my journey in life, I have encountered many men looking for the path that leads to wholeness, wellness, purposefulness, productivity and prosperity. Intuitively most men are aware that such a path does indeed exist. But with no strong male examples to follow and lacking the skills that are necessary to properly research and study such an issue, most males drift through life aimlessly never accomplishing positive goals nor reaching their full potential.

This book, *On the Road to Manhood*, is an effective tool that will not only answer essential questions many men have, but will provide a clear map for entering that path and successfully traveling it. To achieve that goal this book will assist the careful reader to begin finding the way towards understanding himself. There are few lessons in my life that have had more resonance within the deeper places of my soul, than the profound, priceless message locked in the words of that "weeping prophet," Jeramiah, who made that often quoted and pride-less confession, revealing a degree of vulnerability rarely matched in this age, *"Oh Lord, I know that the way of man is not in himself, it is not in man that walks to direct his own steps"* (Jerimiah 10:23).

It saddens me that I spent so many years living recklessly, outside of a properly developed faith. When I consider how far away from the Lord I was, I am blessed that God did not allow death to usher me into the grave, while I wandered aimlessly in sin. It was not until after I had slid down that slippery slope from prominence, as it were, to despicableness, I discovered how very little I knew about truth, reality, good or God. One day it occurred to me, as I pondered Jeramiah's struggle that I, myself, was ill-prepared for the life of godly peace and power, because I was living under the illusion that I knew that vital something about manhood, with which I was only vaguely familiar.

Have you ever been in that place in your own mind? That frame of mind where you think you know more than you really do; but you don't know that you don't know? Where because of your proximity to a truth, you think you know the truth? I am referring to that awful place of deception, where the enemy of our faith has tricked you into a sense of false peace and ease. A place where you even think that everything is just fine, everything is alright, while in reality you may be living in the far country, outside of Christ, disconnected from the God of heaven, and really only a step away from destruction. You ever been there?

Well thank God if you have not, but if any of you, like me, have been anywhere near that dark place, then you know what false peace feels like. And then, maybe you also know how it feels when your eyes begin to open to the reality of your predicament, I most certainly do. When you begin to experience the feelings associated with being lost, hopeless, empty. You know the pain, the hurt that floods a lonely soul, when you realize what you have done to yourself, when you see what has become of you.

I can tell you from my own experience, that there is not a moment quite like that moment when all pride is thrown aside, when the blinders fall off, and just for a moment you can see a truth that had previously alluded you. God had been bringing you to this moment (he sure did me), but pride and sin kept getting in the way, keeping me from seeing it. And then it hits you all at once, as if a loud speaker goes off in your mind, when you finally get it clear in your mind that life is meant to be more than the life I am living.

What a hard pill this can be to swallow, especially for the individual who has become accustomed to not seeing or facing himself. As well for the one who does not yet know or understand the powerful truth in the simple phrase, I am nothing, absolutely nothing without God.

Easy to say right? Is that what you are thinking? I know how often I have made that statement and told others, I am nothing without him, nothing, without God. It makes for good conversations, good for religious talk in Bible classes. I have heard it time and again in popular songs, seen it play out in movie scripts and in books, where the leading character goes through some unprecedented struggle on his way to the realization that life is not worth living without God. But even more to the point, without God the life we have is not really life, but a kind of living death.

Our Lord said it concisely and best, *"Seek ye first the kingdom of God and its righteousness and all these things will be added unto you"* (Matthew 6:33). That statement is often quoted and discussed by godly people, still it seems that few get it. Jesus' words are not simply some suggestion of a course in life among several other options. Quite to the contrary, he is in this profound statement giving *the only solution and the only path* in life one can travel if he wants to discover and uncover on his journey what makes life worth living. Indeed, it is the only path for finding the true peace that comes from God; and it is the only path where victory in Christ can be found.

But what does it mean? And how can we discover the path and know as we travel through life that we remain on the course that leads to life in the kingdom of God? It is this very question I never asked. I am not certain many years ago, before being incarcerated if I even knew to ask it. And that is quite strange itself as I ponder the issue. One day I was working in the church, leading men and women in the ministry of Christ as I understood it at that time. A few seemingly disconnected and innocent decisions later, I was engulfed in a world of ungodliness that lead me down a path towards a slippery slope, culminating in me living in prison and having to survive in an upside-down world.

In my life, I have learned that the most significant challenge to maintaining faith in God through Christ, is in knowing seven fundamental things about life. Having answers to the basic questions concerning the life we have and the life we are meant to live is a vital ingredient to successful living.

Seven Primary Questions of Humanity

These seven questions are said to be primary to humanity, because most every human being on life's journey entertains these seven issues either directly or indirectly throughout his/her life time. It is to the extent that these questions are answered adequately and accurately that a person is able to be fully human and properly engaged in the human experience as intended by the Creator. Our answers to these questions speak to the issue of whether we understand what it means to be truly human.

To be human is to have a mind to think and reason, to have emotions of happiness and sorrow, joy and sadness, love and hate. To be human one can feel compassion for others by expressing sympathy or empathy. Or be uncaring and indifferent. To be human is to love others in many ways through our friendships, family, spouse and our Creator. To be human is to laugh and cry, dream of the future, remember the past, and plan for a better tomorrow.

Many things are attached to this word human. Human kind has been given the power through our Creator to create or invent; to make the world a better world or to cause destruction upon the earth. A human is the most powerful being that our Creator placed on the earth to control our world that is inhabited by many other lower forms of life. Our Creator gave humans the ability to think, ask questions and find answers, to solve problems.

Some of these are things we know inherently. And because we do, we are ever in search of answers to the full meaning of life. Wherever we turn in the books we read, the TV programs, movies we watch, on the news, in schools and colleges, people are trying to find the answers to these question, even though we are rarely asking the questions directly. *On the Road to Manhood*, answers these questions from several aspects, providing the reader practical answers that are life directing. Each question is linked with a key phrase, which, as the phrases are connected

23

together open a wealth of life-giving information that is a helpful formula for directing one's steps on the pathway of life. Pay careful attention to the fact that each question and its adjoining phrase is progressive, one thought building upon the other.

1. What is my origin? Divine Culture creates identity
2. Who am I? Identity inspires purpose
3. Why do I exist? Purpose prescribes function
4. What am I intended to do? Function fosters relationship
5. With whom am I interrelated? Relationship recovers family
6. With whom am I permanently well connected? Family fosters kingdom
7. What is the priority of my life? Kingdom is the urgency of life

These are the issues with which humanity is preoccupied. In most every sector of higher learning, these questions and the issues each exposes are being offered, tested and demonstrated through some media. People everywhere and groups of various kinds and beliefs are attempting to arrest attention so as to persuade us to accept and adopt various conflicting approaches to living. This formula provides a safe plan for finding answers that are biblically based and centered in the wise counsel that comes from years of applying the principles in *On the Road to Manhood*, among people totally disconnected from even basic traditional values.

1: What is my origin? Man has the need to know the very existence. Without knowing this, I will feel lost and out of place, wondering through life confused and disconnected with my world. Divine Culture creates identity! This is the question of the origin of man, which secular society has all wrong. Despite popular theories to the contrary, the Almighty, Everlasting, Sovereign God is the Creator of heaven and earth. I am from the One God and Father of all, Yahoveh. I have neither life nor reason for existence apart from him. He has prescribed a divine culture to make me into the man he designed.

I exist because of my Creator. He and He alone has set up the divine culture that humanity must operate in to live life as it is meant to be. Belief in the Creator of the Bible comes from the knowledge of him that he has provided through the Word of God. God our Father has spoken to man in the Bible, the Word of God, about this life of ours. This information is the basis for the Divine Culture. This culture gives clarity into how we are to live; how we are to think; how we behave; how we form customs; our values in life; our attitudes about life itself and the traditions we form to define ourselves. The Divine Culture of our "Almighty, Everlasting, Sovereign God," our Creator as manifested through Christ Jesus our Lord is the only way of being and living. He is the One who designed us for his purposes and his glory.

Most every problem in this world is directly related to people refusing to accept that the God of heaven is the Creator of this world: The Bible declares, "The earth is the Lord's and the fullness thereof; the world and they that dwell therein" (Psalm 24:1). The true meaning of life can never be fully realized until we accept the Creator God and surrender to his sovereign authority.

2: Who Am I? – What is my true identity? Identity inspires purpose. For so many the question of identity is asked very late in life. Men in prison who are the product of generations of people from backgrounds who have no concept of God. Many of these individuals are unchurched men and women, who have no knowledge of the Creator of the Bible. When one does not know God, that man can never fully know himself. His opinions of himself will always be distorted. The information of who he is will always be incomplete. Furthermore, often many of the things he does know about himself can be largely inaccurate.

Do I know who I am? That is the question each human must ask. But more precisely we must ask, "Is my self-knowledge based on a secular worldview? Is who I am or believe myself to be based on a secular, worldly cultural opinion? Or is my identity born out of a knowledge of who God, my Creator defined me to be in his Word? Those are the series of questions you must ask. And another question, am I who God said I am?

When we do not know our origin, we are destined to have an incorrect opinion of ourselves. This ultimately leads to developing false identities with no proper way for knowing critical things about ourselves, why we act the way we do, why we present ourselves to others the way we do, and feel the way we do, talk the way we talk, enjoy the things of this world that we enjoy, believe what we believe, value what we value, love who we do and how we do. Who we are has everything to do with who our God is. Only as we get to know him can we began to know ourselves.

I know who I am! This has not always been so. And only through the struggles of my life did I even get interested in asking the question concerning my identity. There is nothing like trouble, pain, hurt and deep seated problems that get you to the point where you turn to God for answers to address the problems you are having within yourself, even with yourself.

Who Am I? – What is my true identity? I am a created human being, a man/woman made in the image and likeness of God. My true identity is in being the person the Creator designed and intended for me, which is created in me by learning from and living in the Divine Culture. God created me, in his image, his likeness, his resemblance. The Creator designed me for his purpose. All that is within me has everything I need to learn and live in the Creator, Father God's Divine Culture. He is the only One who can define who I am for his Divine Culture. Only in him can I know who I am.

3: Why Do I Exist? What is my purpose? Why do I live? What is the reason for being alive? We all have a need to know why we are living. Was it by accident that we came to be or by design? Was your birth on purpose? How did you come to be?

Man was made for companionship with the Creator. This is the first and most fundamental of all man's relationships. The idea of having God as a companion is foreign to most men. Rarely do we think of God in this fashion. God, in fact, is depicted this way throughout the Old Testament Scripture. In his relationship with such characters as Abraham, Moses, and David to name a few, God clearly established a relationship that went far beyond simply being their God.

In fact, Abraham is referred to in Scripture as being God's friend (James 2:23). King David is referred to as being a man after God's Own Heart (1 Samuel 13:14, Acts 13:22). And one cannot study the relationship between Moses and God and not be impressed with how unique it was. God spoke to Moses directly, working through him to defeat the king of Egypt. God allowed Moses to come into His very presence so that when Moses returned from the mountaintop with God, his face literally glowed in a manner that caused fear among the people (Exodus 34:29).

The fact that so many men grew up with neither a human father nor a proper father figure makes their relationship with God, as our heavenly Father, even more significant. One of the essential roles of Jesus as the Son of God, is to show us how we can and should interact with our God as our Eternal Father. Jesus made the sacrifices of his life not simply to save us from our sins, which was most certainly primary; but also, to restore fellowship between God and man so that once again we can enjoy the relationship God intended, when he created man from the beginning. In this sense it is important to recognize that we were made for companionship, partnership, and friendship with God. A man who does not have a human father can learn vital and practical information about being a father to his own children, as he establishes through Christ a relationship with the heavenly Father and does his part to remain in harmony with the God of heaven. This results in the formation of a relationship between God and man that will flourish and grow.

It is vital to a proper view of what it means to be a man to understand the relationship between God and man. In discussing roles between the Divine and the human, the Bible teaches that the head of Christ is God, the head of man is Christ, and the head of the woman is the man." But then an astonishing statement is made, "A man ought not to cover his head (when he prays), since he is made in the image and glory of God; but the woman is the glory of man (1 Corinthians 11:7). Man is at the center of God's creative activity. Such a prominent position clearly demonstrates how closely to himself God regards man. This begins to explain why, at the creation of man, God said, "Let us make man in our own image and after our likeness: and let them have dominion over the fish of the sea, and over the fowl of the air, and over the cattle, and over all the earth, and over everything that creeps upon the earth" Genesis 1:26.

This profound statement gives insight into the Divine mindset. It reveals, among other things the value God places on a man; why the Bible indicates that man is "precious" in God's sight (Psalm 116:15); and why God placed such a premium on the soul of a man that it required the sacrifice of his only Son, Jesus, to redeem the human family. Every man should replace any distorted ideas about God, which views him *only* as the Eternal Judge and executor of judgment, who will one day in his wrath punish sinners for their sins, with these facts about God's love for him.

In my own experience the idea that our God is awesome and Mighty took on new meaning, as I begin to comprehend the enormity of his love for me. I did not make the mistake of others who went to the opposite extreme while considering the love of God. Many erroneously conclude that a God of such profound love would not one day execute judgment against Satan, the fallen angelic host, and upon rebellious mankind on account of sin. My understanding about God is tempered by warnings throughout the Scripture against a complacency that leads to acceptance of sinful lifestyles as being unavoidable and therefore permissible. The Bible says, ***"Behold therefore the goodness and severity*** *of God: on them which fell, severity, but toward you, goodness, if you continue in his goodness: otherwise you shall be cut off" (Romans 11:22).*

God's is Holy. His righteousness must and will one day require judgment against those who refuse to repent and accept his kindness in Christ Jesus, which he has given freely to the entire human family as a solution for the problem of sin.

That said, the fact of God's love for me strengthened my grasp and view of him as my heavenly Father and my Eternal Friend. God's love for me is such that he extends levels of grace and mercy to cover my sins and provide me with the tools and divine assistance needed to grow in that grace and live thereby. Unfortunately, my own sons are grown with children of their own, so this new insight will not benefit them in the way it would have had I known these things during their childhood. Still, the information here will assist them to become better fathers and help their sons avoid some of the pitfalls on the road to manhood. Every man needs this broader understanding of God to become the man he was created to be.

Not only man made for companionship with God, but he was intended to exercise dominion over the earth, rulership over himself in union with his mate and fellowship with his physical and spiritual families. Why? To permit man to represent God on this earth to the glory and honor of our God and Father of all. Man was made to have a close relationship with the Creator. This relationship involves intimacy and intercommunication with the Creator the Almighty God our Father. What is a man's purpose in this life? He has a need to know what he is to be and do with his life in order to have a clear picture of his goals and visions, so he can get busy doing what God intended for him to do. The remainder concepts require less explanation when this fact is clarified and established in a man's heart. Below are comprehensive statements, the further discussion of which are outside the scope of this work:

4: What Am I Meant to Do? This question is about function. Man was designed to be an active participant in the work of God, the growth, development and maintaining of himself, family and others using the specific natural talents, spiritual gifting's, and the things in life about which he is passionate to accomplish divine goals, while achieving success to the fullest extent of his potential.

Among the questions a man should ask is "Who has similar interests as I?" As for me, I long for a strong connection to the ones who are supposed to be in my life and a part of my life, even if it is only temporary. These are special people who have the same visions, dreams or mindset as I. We are both heading in the same direction of life and can share ideas together, even if it is just for a short period of our lives.

5: With Whom Am I Interrelated? This is the question about relationship. Through properly focused activities a man interacts directly with other like-minded individuals in ways that help him to maintain objectivity for forming healthy, positive relationships that are mutually advantageous and that empower him to reach divine goals.

6: With Whom Am I Permanently Well-Connected? This is the question about family. By maintaining positive, healthy relationships as a way of life, a man is predisposed toward the recovery and wellbeing of his family, for whom he is responsible and to whom he is wholly accountable to live and be the man the Creator designed and intended.

With whom am I permanently connected? A man has the need to know after sharing his visions and plans with so many, who will be his lifelong friends in his visions and plans. Each man must ask, "With whom will I make life-long connections? Who will be with me until the very end of my life?"

7: What is the priority of my life? This is the question about the Kingdom of God. With and in a stable God conscious family a man is able to seek the Kingdom of God and its righteousness, which is the primary reason for man's existence and is the only path through which a man can find the fulfillment and satisfaction in life for which he longs and seeks after. What is most important in life? While there are so many things in life that are important, each man needs to know what among life's priorities stands out to be most important out of them all. Jesus answered this question when he said, "Seek you first the kingdom of God and its righteousness and all these things will be added unto to you" (Matthew 6:33).

Introduction

Every male has a God given right to transition from boyhood across the divide that leads to manhood. There is a reasonable expectation in civilized society that family structures will accomplish this important task. A powerful biblical statement speaking to the process of male development suggests, "When I was a child, I spoke as a child, I understood as a child, I thought as a child: but when I became a man, I put away childish things."[1] Yet many, through no fault of their own, denied the privilege of this right, are forced to come of age without acquiring the tools needed to function well in a man's world. This is the unfortunate consequence of broken homes, missing fathers, unprepared mothers, and a host of other cultural factors that combine to have a predictable negative impact, stunting the growth of unsuspecting males.

Such a male comes to the place on his life's journey where because of age he must choose a course, a life direction. But he does not know this choice is about the different directions of life. Neither does he know he must choose wisely if he is to become a whole man. Thus, the male makes poor decisions and arrives on the stage of an adult world underdeveloped and unprepared to take a proper role in the unfolding drama of his own life.

Three facts emerge from this familiar dilemma:

A: To be a male is not to be a man

The male attempting to be a man without proper affirmation must fall short. Every immaturity and weakness he has will eventually be exposed. Failure comes mostly because of a lack of information, understanding, and disciplines that shape a real man's character. It is very hard for a so-called "grown man", who is in fact an under developed male, to face this disturbing fact. Indeed, he

---

[1] 1 Corinthians 13:11

33

may look like a man, be viewed by society as being a man, and the reality of his manhood may have never been seriously challenged. But he is not yet a man. Consider the following:

1: Age—Manhood cannot be ascribed by law

Many adult aged males, even some males well advanced in years, never fully developed into a whole man. Just because a male reaches the age where society deems and treats him as a grown man does not mean he is a man.

2: Physical prowess—Manhood cannot be demanded by force

Many males with well-defined physical abilities never fully developed into a whole man. The fact that one is physically strong and capable of doing a man's deeds and duties throughout society does not mean he is a man.

3: Cultural positions—Manhood cannot be assigned by position or title

Many males have responsibilities in society reserved for men. These males operate in various roles as fathers and leaders in many capacities, trying to do a man's work, but never having fully developed into a whole man.

Throughout this document a male not yet affirmed is referred to as a **_male-boy_**. This term is not meant to be derogative, but it is used as a way of calling attention to the fact that a male not yet affirmed, regardless of his age, is still a "boy." This fact accounts for why so many male-boys fail in learning environments that assume a level of emotional maturity from the participant. It also explains why so many are incapable of using tools that permit them to compete in the market place with affirmed men.

Furthermore, it sheds light on why so many are emotionally ill-equipped to function adequately in intimate relationships with mature women or to be responsible parents. The point cannot be overstated: A **MALE-BOY**, which is an un-affirmed male, cannot learn a man's lessons nor bear a man's responsibilities.

B: *Affirmed men must affirm and assist others to achieve manhood*

Fathers who have achieved male affirmation across the divide to manhood are best suited to teach and train other males to make the transition. Involvement in dysfunctional living and criminal activity severely hindered the ability of many natural fathers to rise to the challenges they faced. However, protracted periods of incarceration have given some of these males the space to find safer and better paths to continue their journey. Experiencing the loss of individual freedom and the other negative consequences felons face, often serves as a wakeup call for those who grow weary of the "game" associated with a negative lifestyle. This causes some to seek change and take advantage of every opportunity to grow. After years of participation in prison programming and other self-help studies, many of these men are released from prison hopeful of a better life.

Men who find redemption in or out of a prison environment are uniquely positioned to become mentors and are able to help meet the special needs of other broken males. In fact, because of their former lifestyles, ex-convicts usually relate in ways with those of a common background and experience that other men, who have not walked in their shoes, can find difficult to understand.

An incident during the ministry of Jesus involved a man who is described as being more possessed with demons than any other person Jesus encountered. [2] The man was cutting himself, was very violent, and was living in a graveyard. Interestingly, after Jesus touched him, the man washed, dressed and was observed sitting calmly in his right mind. The man requested to follow Jesus with his other disciples, but Jesus refused to allow him to follow. Jesus instructed the man to "...Go home to your friends, and tell them what great things the Lord has done for you, and has had mercy on you."[3]

Consider the following four points:

1. This man was possibly in the worst spiritual condition of any person Jesus saved.

2. His troubles were greater than many others and he had been saved from so much.

3. Because of how far he had come in being raised up, he was likely prepared in ways that the other disciples were not to go immediately into helping others. Jesus said once, "For unto whomsoever much is given, of him shall be much required: and to whom men have committed much, of him they will ask the more."[4]

4. Perhaps this man had received more than the others. He was ready to serve in a manner that others, even some of Jesus' closest apostles were not. When a person has come out of the darkest places in life, then his unique experiences can equip and position him to go almost immediately to help lift others who are still trapped and unable to find the way of escape.

People of faith rely mostly on simple biblical truth and Christian tradition to explain male growth. In the Bible, a strong emphasis is

---

[2] Mark 5: 1-20
[3] Mark 5:19
[4] Luke 12:48

placed on the role of fathers in directing the maturity of their sons. It takes a man to affirm another male.

This truth is confirmed in the following biblical statements:

1. *"Iron sharpens iron, and one man sharpens another."*[5]

The most obvious point is not lost in this analogy that compares man with iron.

In ancient times when this statement was written, iron was the hardest metal known to man. In a male-driven society, man was considered the strongest being of all. As an iron blade grinds against iron, or against a stronger metal or substance, it can be sharpened to a fine point. Even so, in the counsel and in the give and take exchange among males, a strong, affirmed man has the metal to help other males recover from failures and reach their God-given potential.

2. *"Let not the old landmark be moved which your fathers have put in place."*[6]

This statement illustrates the abiding results of the activities of faithful fathers when they leave clear signpost and markers for their upcoming sons to follow. An important work of fathers is to lay the good foundations of a righteous, godly life in their sons, filling them with the hope of blessings, peace, productivity and prosperity that await those who live by God's standards. These strong human foundations serve as internal landmarks for male-boys that cannot be removed without severe consequences. This explains the wise suggestion in the proverb that says, "Train up a child in the way he should go and when he is old he will not depart from it."[7]

---

[5] Proverbs 27:17
[6] Proverbs 22:28
[7] Proverb 22:6

3. "For this reason the Lord has said, See, I will put stones in the way of this people: and the fathers and the sons together will go falling over them; the neighbor and his friend will come to destruction."[8]

This statement illustrates the sad state of affairs where fathers have led their sons into objectionable standards of living that do not produce life. Such fathers go in the ways that lead to destruction and their sons follow.

4. "And, you fathers, do not make your children angry: but bring them up in the nurture and admonition of the Lord."[9]

In this passage, fathers are encouraged to temper themselves in the manner they deal with their sons so as to not break their spirit: highlighting the goal of a father's work to look after, cultivate and warn their sons, while raising them to manhood.

5. "I have sent a letter to you, fathers, because you have known through experience him who was from the beginning. I have sent a letter to you, young men, because you are strong, and the word of God is in you, and because you have overcome the Evil One."[10]

This passage makes an interesting contrast between a man and a boy. On the one hand, the father has crossed the divide and gained an experiential understanding of life. On the other hand, the son is strong but lacks the experiential knowledge about life that can only be acquired over time. One implication in the verse is that the father provides knowledge the son requires, thereby enabling the son to do what strength demands.

*6. "You **therefore, my son, be strong in the grace that is in Christ Jesus. And the things that you heard of me among***

---

[8] Jeremiah 6:21
[9] Ephesians 6:4
[10] 1 John 2:14

many witnesses, commit those things to faithful men, who shall be able to teach others also." [11]

Those who receive a helping hand out of the Male Wasteland should be willing to share the valuable life lessons they learned, the blessings they received and the new life they enjoy in order to help others cross The Male Divide. Spiritual mentors must hold two important values:

Mentors must be faithful men

Faith is the most reliable quality a person must have to work with God and raise up other men. The Bible declares that "without faith it is impossible to please God."[12] The strength of a man is in the stability of his faith.

Mentors must also be able to teach others

Willingness is ineffective without ability. This powerful statement calls for personal preparation. Mentors must be adequately equipped to teach others.

C: The role of spiritual mentoring is to reverse the affects of failure

Each individual is responsible for the decisions he makes and what he does with his choices in life. Assigning blame when analyzing the consequences of male failure is tempting, but it often yields very little direction for the individual struggling to find a new and better course in life. Besides, overall blame for so much failure with certain male groups can be connected to broad societal failures, traditional familial failures, and a host of neglects and abuses that shed light on the roots of many of the problems so many males have in attempting to reach manhood.

---

[11] 2Timothy 2:1, 2
[12] Hebrews 11:6

One relevant noteworthy issue is how to reverse the negative impact of the failures of individuals who are genuinely seeking change. A central focus in this work is the failures of natural fathers whose primary role directly impacts the development of males. Spiritual mentors serve as fathers and mature brothers. They establish relationships of trust with their peers by modeling the change and maturity broken men long for. The respect they earn helps break down barriers and positions these spiritual fathers/mature brothers to provide some of the positive leadership that many natural fathers did not.

Two points come to light:

1: Spiritual mentoring is a way to start working with a male where he is, not where (it is believed) he should be

Unrealistic expectations imposed on underdeveloped males heighten stress levels and can increase the pressures that bred discouragement. An important aspect of spiritual mentoring is that the tendency toward profiling and not dealing with each man as an individual is minimized. These spiritual fathers were once in the position as the males they now serve and know the importance of accepting each man the way he is and where he is on his life journey.

In the parable of the talents [13] Jesus outlined several layers of proper expectation. The ruler in the parable gave three servants money, called talents, to invest while he was away on a trip. He gave one servant five talents, gave two talents to the second servant, and gave one talent to the third. While the ruler was away, two servants doubled their money with wise investments. However, the servant with just one talent buried

---

[13] Matthew 25:14-30

it, made no investment, and was punished by the ruler when he returned.

Five important lessons should be highlighted:

1. Ruler had a sensible expectation that a proper investment be made.

2. The servant made a critical and incorrect judgment about his ruler. He thought that the ruler, "...reaped where he had not sown" (verse 24). In other words, he was under the impression that the ruler expected to get something for nothing. This was incorrect. The ruler was concerned with the amount of money the servant made.

3. The ruler awarded effort. The unfaithful servant was punished for doing nothing with the talent he had been given.

4. If the servant's opinion of his ruler had been correct, that should have made him work to do the best he could. Instead, he did not even try to do what he could to help himself.

5. It took more effort to dig in the ground and bury his talent than it would have taken to invest it in the market place.

There is a powerful principle in the Word of God concerning what is expected of a person when he is asked to give of himself or his means: "For if there is a ready mind, a man will have God's approval in the measure of what he has, and not of what he has not."[14] A person should never be expected to give what he does not have. The place to begin is always right where one is.

---

[14] 2 Corinthians 8:12

2: Spiritual mentoring is a way to give each person the opportunity to participate in the development of others as a means of helping himself

God seeks men who are willing to help others do right. Consider the following verses:

1. "And I sought for a man among them that should make up the hedge (repair the wall), and stand in the gap before me for the land, that I should not destroy it: but I found none. Therefore, have I poured out mine indignation upon them; I have consumed them with the fire of my wrath: their own way have I paid upon their heads, says the Lord God." [15] "For the eyes of the Lord run to and fro in all the whole earth to show Himself strong on behalf of those whose heart is perfect toward him." [16]

Much of the destruction that happens among men is preventable, but it takes "grown men" to help others find the way across The Male Divide. God is making investments in men who want to help others.

2. "And the Lord said, Simon, Simon, behold, Satan hath desired to have you, that he may sift you as wheat: But I have prayed for you, that your faith fail not: and when you are converted, strengthen your brethren." [17]

This verse presents a simple proposition: when one is converted (which includes the fact that he is raised up from the Male Wasteland and is blessed to get beyond some of the negative lifestyle that was harmful); he can help others find the

---

[15] Ezekiel 22:31
[16] 2 Chronicles 16:9
[17] Luke 22:31, 32

strength needed to rise above negative lifestyles. Spiritual mentoring involves three important values:

A: Mutual submission

"Submit to one another in the fear of God." [18] Spiritual mentoring involves forming a community of men who humble themselves among one another to serve the best interest of all. No force on earth is greater than the power of men who come together in love and unity. The Bible declares, "Behold, how good and how pleasant it is for brethren to dwell together in unity!" [19] Spiritual mentors are men who out of genuine brotherly love desire to see others make real progress beyond their brokenness. To be a mentor is to be:

1) *a big brother*—one who regards others as family for whom he has the concern that a big brother has for his younger brother, taking the safety and well-being of his younger brother as his personal responsibility

2) *a friend*—one who seeks the best interest of another whom he holds in affection, respect, or esteem or whose companionship and personality are important to him

3) *a coach*—one who trains intensively by detailed instruction, frequent demonstration, and repeated practice

---

[18] Ephesians 5:21
[19] Psalms 133:1"

An effective mentor has to operate on some level in all three of these capacities to gain the proper respect of those he serves.

B: Mutual responsibility

"Bear one another's burdens and so fulfill the royal law." [20] Spiritual mentoring involves a united effort on behalf of the entire community, including the individual being mentored. Sharing the load makes everyone responsible for reaching goals; makes each person responsible for everyone else on some level; makes everyone involved in the things that matter to each person's wellbeing; and makes the community more people-oriented and less program- oriented. Each person assumes some responsibility for his brother's success and takes some part in helping keep his brother from failing.

C: Mutual benefits

"Give, and it shall be given unto you; good measure, pressed down, and shaken together, and running over, shall men give into your bosom. For with the same measure that ye mete withal it shall be measured to you again." [21] Spiritual mentoring is an opportunity to help others reach positive goals. The sacrifices one makes on behalf of another are not without challenge or difficulty. However, when a person makes progress and reaches important goals, then those sacrifices take on new meaning for both the individual and his mentor(s). Every investment one makes in the interest of his brother is good for both the recipient and giver. Those who share the

---

[20] Galatians 6:2
[21] Luke 6:38

responsibilities will also share the benefits of the things they do to help others. It has been rightly said that "you cannot help another without also helping yourself."

The Rite of Passage: Understanding Male Affirmation

The rite of passage is connected with the natural stages of life in which a boy reaches the age of social maturity, where he is expected to assume the responsibilities of a man. The crisis of age itself propels him to this point of transition. A boy need do nothing but advance in age and he will naturally reach the stage where because of his age and physical statue, he will be expected to take his place in society. Safe passage toward male affirmation involves teaching and training in the characteristics, beliefs, behaviors, and forecast of a boy's future consistent with manhood.

Male affirmation involves a process of growth that happens in at least six interrelated areas discussed later in the book. It is important to discuss the mutual aspects of these characteristics, in order to emphasize the manner in which these combine to affirm the manhood of an aspiring male. Male affirmation is critical to the wholeness and well-being of a male. When a male who has come of age is adequately affirmed, he is in a good position to be validated, made firm, and thereby able to be secured as a man. Male affirmation contributes significantly to several positive traits of a whole man. When these qualities are modeled for males, they learn by example the strength of character a male must have to reach manhood. At least eight traits are highlighted:

1. *Self-confident*—confidence in one's own strength or ability

2. *Self-asserting*—assertion of one's own rights or claims

3. *Self-controlling*—control over one's passions and emotions

4. *Self-defending*—defense of oneself or belongings

5. *Self-determining*—capacity to self-determine one's own acts

6. *Self-respecting*—respect for oneself and worth as a human being,

7. *Self-sacrificing*—ability to sacrifice oneself for others

8. *Self-supporting*—independent support of oneself

On the other hand, males who reach adulthood without having been affirmed often lack some of these positive traits. If they were not adequately influenced by positive role models, then these males are more inclined to develop several negative traits that contribute to dysfunctional living patterns.

At least five traits are highlighted:

1. *Selfishness*—concern for one's own welfare, advantage or pleasure at the expense of or in disregard of others
2. *Self-centered*—concern solely with one's desires, needs, or interests
3. *Self-importance*—an exaggerated estimate of one' own importance, opinion or merit
4. *Self-justifying*—an automatic seeking to excuse oneself
5. *Self-willed*—not yielding to the ideas, wishes or opinions of others

When male affirmation takes place in the proper course of a boy's life, he should pass through the early life stages with adequate physical, cognitive and social development foundations that will allow him to move successfully into adulthood. Fortunately, missing characteristics of an adult male are attainable, even at a later stage in life. Assuming the male is willing to make a strong personal investment in being taught and trained in the ways of a man. It is never too late to complete the rite of passage to male affirmation. But the challenges of identifying and overcoming thinking errors and negative behavioral patterns in order to make lifestyle changes as an adult male are not easy to address.

This highlights the need for a person to do an honest, thorough, even painstaking personal assessment to determine where he is in relation to wholeness. In doing such an inventory, a male must seek specific information and ask difficult questions. Answers should be evaluated by both the individual and his spiritual mentor(s). An important goal of a careful personal examination is to determine the extent to which an individual has developed the strong characteristics of a man mentioned above.

The Fork in the Road: Understanding Failure

Generally, a teenage male in this country approaches the rite of passage as he reaches 18 years of age. If he has stayed on the "normal" established cultural course, he should complete high school and be positioned to make career choices including college, vocational training, military, or entering the workforce. Many factors are involved in determining which of the available options one chooses. To the extent one has lived in a safe environment, where adults have managed the development of the male, he may have made thoughtful plans giving himself several options when the times comes to decide between paths in life.

All too often, however, this is not the case. The fork in the road is reached prematurely. By the time many male-boys reach this pivotal age, they have already made decisions about becoming parents. Some have also involved themselves in criminal activity and made other adult decisions that have determined their course in life for many years into the future. The very nature of adult decisions, particularly bad decisions, is that consequences are often harsh, difficult to cope with, and irreversible.

The insightful sociological factors that might shed light on how a person likely reaches this critical point in life unprepared for the choices he faces are outside the scope of this work. However, it is significant to suggest an overview of what happens generally to fully explain the role of male affirmation. Such an explanation can also give context for understanding why the investments required for reaching wholeness should not be abandoned by those trapped in the wasteland.

The Male Wasteland is not a physical place but rather a mental, emotional and spiritual disposition. Therefore, it is not surprising how few male-boys find within themselves the courage required to take those first steps toward an exit from this dark place. The lack of self-confidence, peer pressure and fear largely account for why so few make the commitment to do or be better.

As the chart illustrates, a male-boy reaches the fork in the road where he makes one of two choices that will determine his path across The Male Divide. In this visual aid, The Male Divide is viewed as a wide valley situated between two mountainous high grounds. The far left side represents boyhood: the place from which a male-boy coming of age approaches the fork in the road. The far right side represents manhood: the

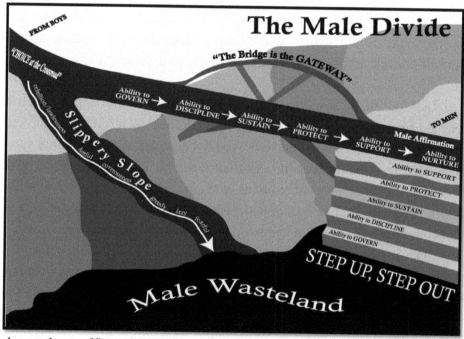

place where affirmed, grown males have successfully crossed the divide from boys to men. At the *Fork in the Road* there is a dangerous path that leads to a Slippery Slope. The *Bridge* provides the safest path for crossing the divide. The divide itself is a vast valley. I call it, **The Male Wasteland.** To the right, inside the Male Wasteland, is the **Step Up, Step Out** path, which is the way out the wasteland.

The *fork in the road* is the determined place every male comes to when he is old enough to make adult decisions. It is a serious time in a young boy's life as some of his decisions are capable of affecting the remainder of his life's journey. The most unfortunate aspect of this place is that it is often determined by variables outside the complete control of the male-boy. This must be so, since one has no choice about the social factors of the environments into which he is born or raised. If that environment is hostile to his proper development, it is conceivable that his life will be pushed along poorly through the adolescent years with a series of events that shape his future in negative ways. Such a male-boy reaches the fork in the road not even realizing he is at that place, making grown-up decisions that lead inevitably to far reaching and often irreversible terrible consequences.

At this critical place in the male-boy's life, his parents should provide instructions and training to help the aspiring male form disciplines for avoiding the pitfalls that lead to the Slippery Slope. Without the influence of a positive father figure or an extraordinarily strong mother, only divine intervention can stop the satanic forces from pulling him down into the Male Wasteland. In reality, it is not just one bad decision that leads to destruction, but one too many mistakes at this critical point that create insurmountable problems.

The path leading to the Slippery Slope and the lifestyle it represents is often a misstep and rarely a conscious decision to choose that lifestyle. Nonetheless, unlike the situation described above, wherein the male-boy is being pushed along by the decisions of others, the male-boy at the fork in the road often makes ill-advised decisions of his own volition and starts down this path; despite the hard working, strong family members that struggle to make every effort to keep their male-boys on the safe path.

But as is discussed in the next section, many male-boys at the fork in the road make choices, sometimes over the anguished pleas of parents, other relatives, and good intentioned friends, to go their own way onto the path that leads to destruction. The Bible teaches that "there is a path before each person that seems right, but it ends in destruction." [22]

Most male-boys never see the magnitude of their wrong choices before the damage to themselves and others has already been done. Only then, after the fact, when they have wreaked havoc in the world and come to a predictable ruin is their eyes opened to the awful mess caused by their decisions. Sadly, quite often the late lesson is learned by the male-boy at the expense of innocent victims left to repair the damages and clean the mess these immature, undisciplined oppressors caused.

This is illustrated forcefully in the parable Jesus told about the prodigal son. [23] In the story, a male–boy having come of age decides to leave home with his father's inheritance and travels to a far country where he gets involved in the street life. It is not long before he is in over his head, out of money, out of friends, alone, with no one to trust and no safe place to go. Sound familiar? His entire adult experience was characterized by the words "loss" and "lack". When he was penniless, hungry and in rags he decided to go back home in the hope that his father would take him in, which the father mercifully did.

This tragic story plays-out with far too many male-boys but without endings as happy as the one in this biblical story. In the streets, male-boys make mistakes that are costly and find trouble that leads to prison. Some behave so poorly that they manage to seriously strain or destroy every good relationship they do have among family and friends. Despite conditions that make the environments in and around one's home unfavorable, there is rarely a situation where a boy has no one around him anywhere to offer a positive alternative to the alluring temptations of the vices and attractions of street life. However, it is true that so many boys with unusual and sometimes seemingly insurmountable obstacles to overcome, given the opportunity of choice, may choose of their own

---

[22] Proverbs 14:12
[23] Luke 11:32

volition and free will the course that leads to destruction. They enter the Male Wasteland alone in the world. And while there is often plenty of blame concerning what went wrong and who contributed to their failures, they are themselves without excuses and must accept personal responsibility for the consequences of the destructive decisions they made.

Once a male-boy starts down this path, reaching the Slippery Slope is almost unavoidable. If he goes too far down that path, he cannot escape unharmed. The phase *Slippery Slope* is used to illustrate the sad reality that once one takes that final step he starts to literally slide down this slope. The decline is steep. The fall is hard. It leads to the worst and most painful and destructive failures conceivable. Most who start down this slope slide all the way down to the very bottom of the pit where they experience drug/alcohol addiction, violent street activity, sexually transmitted diseases, divorce, joblessness, shame, imprisonment, the complete loss of dreams and robbery of their potentials for success, even death. Furthermore, the harm they cause others and the toll on the community is enormous.

Thankfully, our God is the God of second chances. Even in very bad situations and the worst of circumstances there is always *The Way Up*. The statements of hope in the Bible are designed to remind us that the God of heaven and earth, the Creator of all things is in the business of redeeming fallen and broken men who have completely lost their way in life. Consider the following passages:

A. *"For an upright man, after falling seven times, will get up again: but trouble is the downfall of the evil."* [24]

✓ An "upright man" is not a perfect man who never makes mistakes. But one is upright when he decides to turn from his wicked ways and seek the Lord with all his heart. Remember this: being upright is a decision, a personal choice! Therefore, choose to be upright and turn to the Righteous God for direction and "Trust in the

---

[24] Proverbs 24:16

Lord with all your heart and do not lean on your own understanding, but in all your ways acknowledge him and he shall direct your steps." [25]

B. *"If my people, which are called by my name, shall humble themselves, and pray, and seek my face, and turn from their wicked ways; then will I hear from heaven, and will forgive their sin, and will heal their land."* [26] This is a powerful statement of God's willingness to redeem the fallen. Those who honor this Word of God will be "upright" before him. The heavenly formula for being right with God is outlined simply in this verse. Read it; believe it; trust it; and do it!

<u>You do this</u>:
- ✓ *Humble yourself*—do not be prideful, arrogant; but be lowly
- ✓ *Pray*—talk to God about everything; establish prayer times for each day
- ✓ *Seek his face*—desire to be in relationship with him; do not just try to get him to do things for you or to give you things
- ✓ *Turn from your wicked ways*—let go of the lifestyle of your past

<u>God says he will do this</u>:
- ✓ *I will hear from heaven*—God will hear your prayers if you will pray
- ✓ *I will forgive your sins*—God will completely forgive your past
- ✓ *I will heal your land*—God will fix your land, which involves everything and everyone in the place you live. He will

---

[25] Proverbs 3:5
[26] 2 Chronicles 7:14

completely restore you so that you can be peaceful, productive, prosperous, and powerful in the ways God designed you to be.

C. *"But if the evil-doer, turning away from all the sins which he has done, keeps my rules and does what is ordered and right, life will certainly be his; death will not be his fate. Not one of the sins which he has done will be kept in memory against him: in the righteousness which he has done he will have life. Have I any pleasure in the death of the evil-doer? Says the Lord: am I not pleased if he is turned from his way so that he may have life? But when the upright man, turning away from his righteousness, does evil, like all the disgusting things which the evil man does, will he have life? Not one of his upright acts will be kept in memory: in the wrong which he has done and in his sin death will overtake him. But you say, the way of the Lord is not equal. Give ear, now, O children of Israel; is my way not equal? Are not your ways unequal? When the upright man, turning away from his righteousness, does evil, death will overtake him; in the evil which he has done death will overtake him. Again, when the evil-doer, turning away from the evil he has done, does what is ordered and right, he will have life for his soul. Because he had fear and was turned away from all the wrong which he had done, life will certainly be his; death will not be his fate."* [27] *These seven Bible verses gives one of the clearest statements in the Word of God about how God regards sin and under what conditions God will restore a person. It is a powerful statement of who God considers "upright."* Read it; believe it; trust it; and do it!

You do this:

✓ *Turn away from your past lifestyle*

This is a process that takes several steps and time. Change is not easy. Making "real" behavioral changes that involve overcoming habits is often gradual. The important thing that

---

[27] Ezekiel 18:21-28

God requires of you is first _a made-up mind_. God requires you to be fully, completely determined to let go of the past lifestyle that is responsible for your brokenness, your faults, your failures and the pain your actions caused others. Real change begins with a changed mind. You can never change your behavior until you are determined in your mind and heart to change.

✓ *Keep God's rules*

This is a process that takes several steps and time. God requires you to make a commitment first to learn his rules for your life and to begin following your spiritual mentors as they model before you the new lifestyle. Know this: God's rules for life are not complicated. His rules involve Ten Commandments that you can learn and follow if you want to. Jesus said, "As the Father hath loved me, so have I loved you: continue you in my love. If ye keep my commandments, ye shall abide in my love; even as I have kept my Father's commandments, and abide in his love." [28]

✓ *Do what is ordered and right*

Divine order is important. Everything in the world and our lives is established by God's order. Therefore, the Word of God teaches, "*Let all things be done decently and in order.*" [29] The Bible teaches further that, "*The steps of a good man are ordered by the Lord, and he takes delight in his way.*" [30] "Upright men" respect God's order and understand that doing all things right and in order is the way that leads to life, peace, health, productivity, and prosperity.

---

[28] John 15:9, 10
[29] 1 Corinthians 14:40
[30] Psalms 37:23

✓ *Have reverence for the Lord in turning away from all wrong*

Consider two important verses:

1. *"The fear of the Lord is the beginning of knowledge: but fools despise wisdom and instruction."* [31]

2. *"The fear of the Lord is the beginning of wisdom: and the knowledge of the holy is understanding."* [32]

This "fear" is respect. It involves knowing that God is the Almighty, Eternal True, and Living God who alone has all power and all authority in himself! This is the only God worthy of worship and the only One we should give reverence as God. This is the first important lesson we must learn in life to become an "upright" person. We have no knowledge worth knowing, no wisdom worth relying on and no understanding worth trusting until we know that we must reverence the Lord God Almighty! This is the beginning of knowledge, wisdom and understanding.

God says he will do this:

✓ *God will give you life*

Jesus promises, *"I have come so that you may have life and have it in greater measure."* [33] The phrase, *"...give you life,"* involves the quality, the value, the goodness, the excellence in life. God accepts us at the point of our brokenness and, if we will follow his plans and purposes, then he restores the goodness of life to us.

---

[31] Proverbs 1:7
[32] Proverbs 9:10
[33] John 10:10

✓ *Destruction and death will not be your fate*

Your past can be literally redirected and restructured from bad to good in which even some negative consequences and judgments are subject to being changed. *"And I will restore to you the years that the locust hath eaten, the cankerworm, and the caterpillar, and the palmerworm, my great army which I sent among you."* [34]

✓ *God will not hold the past faults and failures against you*

God intends to bring you to the place of perfect peace. This is only possible if you are permitted to make a brand-new start. In reference to your past faults and failures, God proclaimed, *"I, even I, am he who takes away your sins; and I will no longer keep your evil doings in mind."* [35] This is expressed in the good news that, *"...if any man be in Christ, he is a new person: old things are passed away; behold all things are become new."* [36]

✓ *God will allow the righteousness you do now to bring you life*

God uses your faithfulness and participation in making life better for yourself and other men to usher in the life you want and need. Emphasis is placed on the word *"now."* The things you may have done in the past to bring life must be continued every day. Being upright is a lifestyle; it is not a onetime act.

This combination of biblical statements powerfully portrays the fact that the Male Wasteland does not have be the final destination for the male who has fallen down the Slippery Slope. The way up involves taking six key steps that are discussed at length in another section. Each progressive step is on the path out of the Male Wasteland and toward male affirmation.

---

[34] Joel 2:25
[35] Isaiah 43:25
[36] 2 Corinthians 5:17

This path leads out of the pit and across The Male Divide. It is a challenging and difficult place from which to begin building the character of a man. However, it is the path that leads out of the low valley to higher ground.

As the chart illustrates the *Bridge* is the safe way across The Male Divide. Those male-boys who are fortunate enough at the fork in the road to avoid bad choices and bypass the Slippery Slope move onto the bridge toward male affirmation. Still, the critical lessons and training required for male affirmation are the same, whether one is moving across the bridge or climbing out of the Male Wasteland. The good news is that it is never too late. A male's situation is never too bad, where you are right now is always the best place to start, and today is the best time to begin your journey toward wholeness.

The Negative Consequence of Choices: Six Major Male-Character Flaws

In far too many instances, negative consequences are the result of bad decisions. Yet, not all undesirable consequences are created equal. Some naturally are costlier than others. The development of male-character flaws is doubtless among the most common long-term negative consequences of the misdirected decisions made by a male-boy. The more advances a male-boy makes down the destructive path, he must ultimately arrive at the Slippery Slope. Sooner or later on that path he reaches the "point of no return." When he does take that final step, then down into the Male Wasteland he falls. The more engaged in destructive lifestyles he becomes, the longer he remains in the Male Wasteland, and the greater potential damages to his character and harm to others. Real dangers also exist that the longer he stays in the Male Wasteland the greater the possibility he may never recover or find the way out.

There is a difference between a single failure and a pattern of living, a lifestyle. The risk in doing a bad thing even once is great because of how pleasurable sin often is, especially at first. The Bible says about Moses, *"When he was come of age, he refused to be treated like the son of Pharaoh's daughter; choosing rather to suffer affliction with the people of God, than to enjoy the pleasures of sin for a season."* [37] It is common knowledge that the world is full of pleasurable activities. But at what cost to the individual does he partake of the world's false treats? Far too many men now in the Male Wasteland were trapped by the thrills, the highs, the good times, the feelings of happiness that seemed like bountiful pleasures that would never end. But the temporary delights soon give way to pain, hurt and disaster, takings on a life of its own and can last for many years. Such a lifestyle often leaves in its wake a crowd of victims whose lives are disrupted, permanently changed, even ended. These consequences are the

---

[37] Hebrews 11: 24, 25

result of thoughtless individuals whose actions cause such pain and mayhem for others to bear. Again, the Word of God affirms, *"There is a path before each person that seems right, but it ends in destruction."* [38]

Male-character flaws are cultivated gradually over years. In the early developmental stages of life, negative behavioral traits can easily be dismissed as belonging to a temporary phase of life. What we might call a passing fad. But over time repeated acts of wickedness causes patterns of behavior to become a hardened part of an individual's character. Numerous forms of these characteristics are possible and for the most part are different for each person. However, there are six traits common among males who fall down the Slippery Slope into the Male Wasteland.

These six male-character flaws are intentionally ordered below to suggest a specific pattern of failure into the Male Wasteland. The order of these characteristics is designed as a guide to shed light on issues of male brokenness (that may help explain how malfunction expands); to highlight the accumulative effect of vices associated with these characteristics (that may help an individual understand some of the contributing factors involved in how he became the person he is); and to identify the extent to which an individual may have been infected by the negative influences he encountered (that may help make plain the specific steps an individual must take to change unhealthy thinking and behavioral patterns).

1: Rebellious/Lawless

Simply defined, a rebellious person is one operating in opposition to the authority. A lawless person is unruly; one who refuses to be regulated or controlled by law; one who is ungovernable. Rebellion leads to lawlessness. The common factor with all males who choose the path that leads to the Slippery Slope and ultimately to the Male Wasteland is some form of rebellion that gives way to lawlessness. The Bible instructs that

---

[38] Proverbs 14:12

rebellion is the result of *"rejecting the word of the Lord."* [39] Rebellion always involves rejection of the right one person assumes to have over another. But rebellion against the things that are just, right and lawful is always rejection of God's right to influence and rule over us. Rarely is this matter understood in the context of God's right to rule over us, and as a result, the full implications for how a seemingly simple, isolated decision can have a negative impact on one's whole life is not seen.

An important fundamental aspect in the nature of males "coming of age" is the need for self-governance. This is the positive opposite of rebellion. It is proper for a male-boy to seek emancipation from parental restraints and structures. He should long to give full expression to the pursuit of desires and dreams forming in his mind. However, until he has more experience and understanding in and of life not all of his thoughts processes are well conceived. Loving parents or concerned authority figures attempt to keep him focused on plans and goals that will insulate, maybe even, protect him from some of the hazards associated with his desires and dreams. So, a conflict develops that may become bitter, depending on the quality of parental influence/authority and the level of skill they use with the male-boy attempting to make this vital transition to adulthood.

Complicating his position is the extent to which a male-boy is being influenced by other misdirected people, particularly those in his age group, presenting unhealthy choices and flashing perks that make their lifestyle preferable to his own. His internal conflict may also be exacerbated by previous unwise decisions he has made, like the obligations of having prematurely become a parent. Whatever the factor, however, the conflicts as the male-boy comes of age has implications that directly impact his future. When he chooses the path leading to the Slippery Slope, then with pleasure he becomes intolerant of the authority figures that are blocking his path. At that point, it does not take very much of a push on the part of

---

[39] I Samuel 15:23

parents and others for him to rebel against them or for him to move forward toward lawlessness.

Rebellion is the first step down the Slippery Slope. It is the point of no return. In fact, after he rebels, the only matter left unresolved for the male-boy is how far into the Male Wasteland he will fall, which is a matter entirely dependent on how unruly he becomes. Of the male character flaws discussed in this work, rebellion and lawlessness pose the first risk for the male-boy. It is this first step that sets the tone for the other flaws, determining just how deeply entangled in a destructive way of living he will get, and it significantly factors into the level of difficulty he will have transitioning across The Male Divide.

The rebellious individual who enters the Male Wasteland rejects God's right to rule and man's duty to impose and enforce laws that protect society. The language of the rebel is, "I am my own man; I will do what I want, how I want, the way I want, when I want." The language of the lawless is, "I decide what is right or wrong for me; whatever I choose to do is right for me. How you respond to it is up to you. You do you, I'll do me." Such a rebellious and lawless person will sink to the lowest levels of the Male Wasteland at enormous cost to himself and others. Just how low he will go or how much loss he will experience depends greatly on several sociological factors. Needless to say, the individual living in a dysfunctional environment is subjected to greater risk than the one with the good fortune of having been born into a relatively stable background.

2: Lustful

A lawless person reaches a point of spiritual poverty where he practices very few respectable personal disciplines. He gives himself to the hunt of pleasure. The occasional "good time" becomes the routine of a life where entertainment, parties, and fun-filled events take the place of work and the pursuit of positive goals. In the modern world where an almost limitless assortment of entertainment events and a host of things that bring pleasure are available on demand, the sinking person descends to a progressively lower level in the Male Wasteland where he is governed more by his lust than by good sense and sound reasoning. Over time he runs the risk of becoming completely consumed by lust.

A clear signal that the male-boy has not crossed The Male Divide into manhood is in his failure to rule over the natural urges of his flesh. The ability to control one's natural desires is a primary sign of maturity. But keeping ordinary human desires under control is important for another reason. Unlike animals that function solely on instincts, a human's natural desires are connected to body and mind. For example, a human being and a thirsty animal need water for the same reason. The proper function and wellbeing of the body is partly dependent on an adequate intake of water. A dehydrated animal is satisfied with water. But a dehydrated human being may choose a cold bottle of his favorite soda pop, a glass of ice tea, or some other substance other than water to satisfy his thirst. His body has to break down the soda pop to get the water it needs to stay healthy. That person's mind-driven desire for a substance other than water distorts the actual needs of his dehydrated body. Repeatedly choosing liquids other than water over years, especially if he drinks no water at all, could cause ill health.

Distorted desires are dangerous. These unbridled lust open doors in a man's life that lead to the most destructive behavioral patterns possible. The lawless person is mentally positioned to have his natural desires turned into inordinate lust. This type of excessive desire is so strong that a person "throws all caution to the wind" and refuses to deny himself any pleasures he wants. Demonic operations are most active among those who have inordinate lust. Because they practice little restraints, many of these individuals will do almost anything, at least once. Evil spirits roam the earth attempting to inhabit anyone who permit them to gain entrance. But they are particularly interested in the most spiritually vulnerable individuals.[40] For this reason the Bible encourages us to properly prepare ourselves to face and fight the forces of evil working against us:

"Be strong with the Lord's mighty power. Put on all of God's armor so that you will be able to stand firm against all strategies and tricks of the devil. For we are not fighting against people made of flesh and blood, but against the evil rulers and authorities of the unseen world, against those mighty powers of darkness who rule this world, and against wicked spirits in the heavenly realms. Use every piece of God's armor to resist the enemy in the time of evil, so that after the battle you will still be standing firm. Stand your ground, putting on the sturdy belt of truth and the body armor of God's righteousness." [41]

Excessive lust opens an emotional door to direct confrontation with demons. Many male-boys, while under the influence of evil spirits, commit horrible acts seeking to fulfill lusts that can never be fully satisfied. No one should make excuses about their mistakes, while seeking to dismiss personal responsibility for their decisions and deeds. However, in regard to satan, demons, devils, evil spirits, familiar spirits, unclean spirits, these are not imaginary beings conceived by "church people" and discussed in Sunday school to scare us. Satanic activity is very real in this world.[42] The influence of evil spirits does not excuse personal behavior, nor does it dismiss personal responsibility, but it does expose the not-too-obvious spirit powers that influence human choices and decisions. This spiritual conflict is expressed clearly in the following biblical statement:

"And I have no clear knowledge of what I am doing, for that which I have a mind to do, I do not, but what I have hate for, that I do. But, if I do that which I have no mind to do, I am in agreement with the law of sin that it is good. So it is no longer I who do it, but the sin living in me. For I am conscious that in me, that is, in my flesh, there is nothing

[40] 1 Peter 5:8; Luke 11:24-26
[41] Ephesians 6:10-17
[42] Matthew 4:24; 8:16; 8:28-34; 12:42-43; Mark 1:26; 16:9; Luke 8:29; Acts 19:13-15; 1 Corinthians 10:20; James 2:19

good: I have the mind but not the power to do what is right. For the good which I have a mind to do, I do not: but the evil which I have no mind to do, that I do. But if I do what I have no mind to do, it is no longer I who do it, but the sin living in me. So I see a law that, though I have a mind to do good, evil is present in me. In my heart I take pleasure in the law of God; But I see another law in my body, working against the law of my mind, and making me the servant of the law of sin which is in my flesh. How unhappy am I! Who will make me free from the body of this death? I give praise to God through Jesus Christ our Lord. So with my mind I am a servant to the law of God, but with my flesh I obey the law of sin." [43]

Inordinate lust is a subtle trap, because it involves natural desires. Any desire can be distorted and become unnatural. Consider the following list of natural desires we all have that can become distorted and lead to undesirable behavior. Since most of these are desires that for the most part we cannot stop having altogether, once distorted these desires can become an agonizing source of emotional and physical bondage:

- Distorted desires for *food* lead to gluttony
- Distorted desires for *alcohol* lead to drunkenness
- Distorted desires for *leisure* lead to laziness and slothfulness
- Distorted desires for *sex* lead to all types of sexual promiscuity (including fornication, adultery, homosexuality, sodomy, bestiality, prostitution, child molestation, pornography, orgies)
- Distorted desires for *material things* lead to greediness
- Distorted desire for *another man's house* (wife, family, possessions, positions) lead to covetousness
- Distorted desires for *power* lead to ruthlessness and tyranny
- Distorted desires for *preservation* leads to selfishness and self-centeredness

---

[43] Romans 7:15-25

- Distorted desires for *importance* leads to pride

The role of temperance cannot be overstated for the individual determined to rise above the tyranny of humanity's lower passions. The ability to control one's self and maintain personal disciplines that provides safeguards against a wandering mind and a longing flesh must be among our highest priorities. There is an undeniable reality regulating the human family in our present fallen state: the capacity for pleasure has become unquenchable, driving us to turn our highest attentions to a quest for fulfillment of that for which our hearts long. This pursuit once prioritized will not lose steam easily, nor will its resulting shame deter most under its control. Instead it pushes the one held by its promises of pleasure further down into the Male Wasteland introducing him to the next flaw seeking his ruin.

3: Covetous

Covetousness is rooted in a jealousy and envy that provides a path for inordinate lust. It causes one to lose proper affection for what he possesses, preferring instead that which belongs to another. The biblical admonition against this insidious desire and longing is quite emphatic: *"You shall not covet your neighbor's house. You shall not covet your neighbor's wife, nor his servants, nor his ox, nor his donkey, nor anything that is your neighbor's."* [44]

Whether the male-boy covets another man's wife, his belongings, or his successes, he is essentially lusting, whether it is for women or for possessions or status. He is envying and desiring for that which belongs to another, which he has not earned by his responsible acceptance of affirmed male-character. It is an immature vision of pleasure without merit or effort or deservedness. It will speedily misroute him further-yet down the Slippery Slope into the Male Wasteland, where he will wallow hopelessly in his desires and inordinate lusts of every sort. Unfortunately,

---

[44] Exodus 20:17

at this level in the Male Wasteland, the male-boy is exposed to other broken individuals who join together influencing and encouraging each other to seek fulfillment of their lust. This inevitably results in doing harm to some innocent, often unsuspecting, persons who are the objects of their inordinate lust.

Covetousness was one of the human weaknesses that satan sought to prey upon when he tempted Jesus during his time in the wilderness: *"Again, the devil took him up into an exceeding high mountain, and showed him all the kingdoms of the world, and the glory of them; And said unto him, 'All these things I will give you, if you wilt fall down and worship me.'"* Jesus' rejoinder to Satan to *"... get behind me, satan, for it is written, you shall worship the Lord your God, and him only shall you serve,"*[45] clearly makes the key point that to covet and lust for things and power that belong to others is to turn away from God in pursuit of ways that lead only to destruction. The Male Wasteland is full of male-boys who took the seemingly easy path down to it by succumbing to the temptations of the world while taking no responsibility for owning their decisions, preferring instead to own another's possessions. The ability to self-govern and discipline oneself, to rise out of and above inordinate lust and covetousness, as will be covered later, are two key progressive steps on the stairway out of the Male Wasteland toward affirmed, responsible manhood.

The male-boy who is covetous of affirmed male attributes and possessions without wanting to responsibly own them also belittles and ignores his own talents, gifts and potentials God has given him. He remains unaware that he is a male of God. He has chased after everything else except what God implanted in him already in his creation. He is missing the point of life completely.

An important aspect of the biblical story discussed in an earlier section is applicable here. It concerns the servant who received one talent from his

---

[45] Matthew 4:8

master and rather than use it unwisely buried it, made no investment, and was punished by the ruler when he returned. Like him, many fail to see value in the talents they possess. They develop attitudes of jealousy, envy and ultimately become covetous. This results in the rise of an unhealthy discontentment with self and the growth of inordinate desires to stand in another's place. If "burying one's talent in the sand," were the only response of the unmotivated male-boy that would be tragic enough. But this single act would not necessarily inconvenience, disadvantage or harm anyone else. Tragically, however, covetousness, as is discussed below, is just a step or two from another undesirable male character flaw, laziness. As is expressed in the old saying, "an idle mind is the devil's workshop," being idle is the bedrock for a significant amount of the evil deeds in this world. The idle-minded person, filled with covetousness, very often invests himself in the invention of untoward plans that gives rise to an insatiable appetite for another's possessions and positions. It is often this unchecked greed that sets sinister plans into motion. The male-boy is moving further down the slippery slope, and if he is not careful, he may never recover.

4: Greedy

Greediness follows inevitably from covetousness that distorted desire for material things and another man's house. It is the next downward step and the increasingly-destructive trait that arises from lust and coveting things. Also, it is a further progressive step along the Slippery Slope into the Male Wasteland. The male-boy not yet a man is wide-eyed at all that he sees around him, the expensive homes, cars, possessions, clothes, jewelry, even women on the arm, of others around him. He has a child's immature desire to possess the most marbles on the playground of life. Defining and measuring himself largely by his material possessions, he perceives success and self-worth only in the contexts of what looks impressive to others and what improves his standing among that social group. While he is greedy for all the fruits of affirmed manhood and responsible success in the world, he lacks the character to realize that such things are earned and deserved, not simply seized greedily.

Greed is a fundamental human flaw that precipitated the original sin. During the temptation of Eve in the Garden of Eden, she became dissatisfied with herself. Convinced that the tree provided her an opportunity to get what she lacked and that its fruit would fill her void, Eve ate it. The desire she had for more was false, since nothing in fact was missing from her life and Satan's information was wholly untrue in every detail. She had it all and lost it all chasing after something that was not real.

Dissatisfaction is the original emotional sin and it is the birth of greed. Dissatisfaction leads to rebellion and disobedience. It plagues the human family in ways that few other flaws do or can. The Bible states: *"Hell and destruction are never full; so the eyes of man are never satisfied."* [46] There is plenty of room in the place designated for the final judgment of those who do evil. That place, hell, can never be filled to a level where it is not able to receive all who deserve to go there. The desires of most all human beings to gain more and more of the things we see can never be satisfied. For so many "it is never enough," no matter what "it" is. The more money we gain, the more things we get; and the more things we get, the more things we want. For many people it is a never-ending cycle and a sad commentary on the inability of people to find contentment in life.

Jesus illustrated this truth with a parable about a man who had been tremendously successful in his agricultural business. He was confronted with solving the problem of having a bigger harvest than storage space to receive it. In the teaching, Jesus emphasized the need for sharing and self-sacrifice by pointing out the full extent of the man's insatiable desire for things:

---

[46] Pr 27:20

"And he said to himself, 'What is to be done? For I have no place in which to put all my fruit. And he said, this I will do: I will take down my store-houses and make greater ones, and there I will put all my grain and my goods. And I will say to my soul, Soul, you have a great amount of goods in store, enough for a number of years; be at rest, take food and wine and be happy.'" [47]

Rather than consider giving the extra crops he had to the poor and needy, the man decided to build bigger barns and install larger storage bins for his grains and goods. Dissatisfaction leads to greediness, which in turn breeds selfishness, which leads to self-centeredness. So much of a person's lowest traits is born from this root. It makes the person ruled by such attributes easy prey. The lure of evil's enticements to easy access of false promises lead further down into the Male Wasteland of lust, covetousness, and greed. The male-boy taking the path out of the Male Wasteland will, as he climbs the steps upwards toward affirmed manhood, be quite literally striving to rise above his own inordinate desires.

5: Lazy

A rebellious, lustful, covetous, greedy person inevitably develops distorted desires for leisure and pleasure that will lead him further downward into the Male Wasteland toward laziness. The male-boy wants immediately all the rewards of a disciplined life, without displaying any willingness to put in the work to deserve the fruits of responsible male affirmation and success in life. Inevitably, he lacks any sense of work ethic to achieve and earn things through lawful employment or business. More often than not, he did not have responsible male role models growing up. Or, those he did have were ignored in favor of the more glittering qualities seen in friends.

Laziness is part and parcel to an immature desire for undeserved things. It is all about trying to take the short and easy path rather than the

---

[47] Lu 12:16-21

steadier, harder path of responsible life towards the fulfillment of one's goals and dreams. The old adage, "Idle hands are the devil's playthings" is absolutely correct. Idleness and laziness lead straight to an irresponsible and even criminal lifestyle where an "I'm gonna get mine!" mindset prevails. Even if that means taking from others whose belongings or hard-earned success the male-boy covets, feeling that he is somehow "entitled" to such, and that others are stupid to work for such, when they could just take it, as he does. The climb out of the Male Wasteland takes work, plain and simple. It is rising above laziness. "Nothing ventured, nothing gained" is a popular slogan, but more than that, it summarizes well the role of hard work as a prerequisite to success.

Laziness as a character flaw added with covetousness and greed is the combination that precipitates undesirable, unproductive, even hostile behavior. The lazy person suffers lack and loss in direct relation to his slothfulness. A wise proverb says, "Laziness throws one into a deep sleep, and an idle person shall suffer hunger."[48] The Bible also warns, "He who does not give his mind to his work is brother to him who makes destruction."[49] The lazy uninspired individual who refuses to be productive often spends countless hours daydreaming about things he wants to possess, places he would like to go and the social status he longs to have. Through media like television, his endless fantasies are given specific target, which becomes fuel for evil plans and angles burning in his mind to get what he wants. The so-called "easy way" regardless of who gets hurt in the process is his mindset.

This demonstrates the dangerous, accumulative, negative effect these specific male flaws have on the male-boy. Each downward step leads him further away from being a citizen of decent society. Without doubt he soon travels the darker paths and ways of criminal thinking and living. As the young male-boy assimilates into this other world, he is changing in

---

[48] Pr 19:15
[49] Proverbs 18:9

unhealthy ways, often unbeknown to himself, becoming hardened to a criminal lifestyle. Any hopes he held of holding on to childhood dreams of pursuing a certain career, along with the desires held by family members that he would realize his full potential begin to fade away with the passing of each day. Before long it all becomes nearly an impossible dream as each new negative episode of his life seals his fate and like a nail driven into a coffin locks him in a box from which he can hardly escape.

At this point, when it is too late to escape the consequences of a series of bad choices and decisions, when the full weight of loss takes toll on his life, effectively shutting him out of the normal freedoms that cultivate success, his eyes may begin to open to the reality of his brokenness. Whatever personal strengths he once enjoyed, the male-boy at this stage has opened himself to arguably the worst male character flaw of all, *fear*.

Fearfulness robs the male-boy of the ability to become a whole male. It locks him into a dreadful place where it maintains an unrelenting grip on his soul, stripping his spirit of every power needed to rise above the darkness and the negative vices of the Male Wasteland. Once he falls to this point it is all but impossible to avoid the final steps leading to complete ruin in the Male Wasteland.

6: Fearful

At length, as a culmination of all the steps leading progressively downward as set forth above, the male-boy is essentially left a fearful person adrift in a world without markers or guideposts, lost along his way toward any concept of affirmed manhood. His is a fearfulness born of confusion and desperation and hopelessness. He is afraid of crossing the Male Divide because he lacks a male guide or even the concepts necessary to navigate it. Instead of venturing confidently forth across the chasm toward affirmed manhood, he childishly opts for the quick easy path that veers off downwards at the fork in the road. His is a personality and behavior that is all about bluster, posturing, and pretense, rather than confidence and sense of direction and the ability to stand responsibly, as a man, in his own right. Once he reaches the Male Wasteland, as he inevitably will, fear keeps him there. He is embarrassed at his own failure and shallowness, and it is often easier for him to remain where he is than to admit his whole life has been misguided and a failure. It takes real courage to begin the steep ascent out of the wasteland up the six steps to affirmed manhood. By definition, that journey is rising above paralyzing fearfulness to start the climb upward again to reach responsibility and fulfillment as a man.

Fear is the opposite of faith. Faith is the fundamental requirement of humanity that separates us from animals and distinguishes boys from men. A child's faith permits him to move with innocence and simplicity through the challenges of his young life without hesitation, relying on the strengths and good intentions of those who serve as his faith's object. By distinction, a man's faith is not so blind, but it informs every choice and decision he makes. Faith boosters the courage and intestinal fortitude to confront life's challenges in the enduring hope that the object of his faith provides adequate power to achieve victory. In fact, faith is so basic to successful living that the Bible declares, *"Without faith it is impossible to please God; he that comes to God must believe that he is and that he is a rewarder of him that diligently seeks him."*[50]

Fear blocks God as the proper object of faith and replaces him with other people, circumstances and things that are unworthy of the role and incapable of meeting its requirements. *"For we walk by faith and not by sight"*[51] is an important Christian tenet. In contrast to this concept, fear is problem-oriented, focusing one's attention on troubles or obstacles and the many reasons there can be for a person not putting sufficient effort or sacrifice toward reaching his goal. Conversely, faith is solution-oriented. With faith as the source and guide of information, the faith-led person

---

[50] Hebrews 11:6
[51] 2 Corinthians 5:7

75

searches for a way to rise above problems. That faith finds strength for moving beyond protest and prosecution of the problem toward resolution. Fear elevates the problem to a higher position in the person's mind than is proper or necessary. It causes the person to rely on himself, functioning as a god over his own life, considering himself to be more competent and capable than he is or can ever be. Interestingly, Jesus announced that the first prerequisite to discipleship is precisely to denounce one's right to consider himself as a reliable source for leadership, aid or strength in favor of accepting the Lordship of Christ. He said, *"If any will be my disciple let him deny himself, take up his cross and follow me."*[52] The phrase *"deny himself"* has no immediate reference to giving up material things or positions as such. It is a requirement for the prospective disciple to deliberately give up the natural right he has to rule over himself. He becomes another's servant, not by force or coercion, but as an exercise of his own will. The faith-led individual relies on his Lord's help to confront fear and learn to live without its doubts.

---

[52] Matthew 16:24

The Positive Consequence of Choices: Key Characteristics of a Man

Good character is a chief quality of a strong man. It has often been observed that a man may have superior talents, gifts, and advanced skills, such as permit him to win the acceptance of influential people and do great things, but he can lack the character required for holding to the success his gifts afford him. Ultimately the character of a person determines the level of his success. A man with good character will be more accomplished in the things that really matter in life than the man who fails to develop the enduring characteristic of real success.

But what is success? And how is success really determined and measured? Of course, it largely depends on the individual and what he values. Still, a common mistake is made by those who measure success in material terms. To them the more money, material things and positions one gains, the greater successful he is said to have. But many people spend the balance of their lives pursuing material success only to discover at long last that money, material things and status cannot alone provide the joy, peace and happiness in life for which the human soul longs.

On this point, Jesus taught that one should *"Take care to keep yourself free from the desire for property; for a man's life is not made up of the number of things which he has."*[53] Consider also these two thought provoking questions Jesus asked: *"What good will it do a man to gain the whole world, if he forfeits his life? Or what will a man give that is of equal value with his life?"*[54] The history of humanity is full of the stories of so-called successful people who lived the "good life" with all the trappings of success and every privilege reserved for the wealthy but who

---

[53] Luke 12:15
[54] Matthew 16:26

were miserable, lonely failures in relationships. While they are largely hailed as successful, in reality they failed.

Real success involves many non-material things, like the love and respect of others and a good name. The Bible states, *"A good name is more to be desired than great wealth, and to be respected is better than silver and gold."*[55] The qualities an aspiring male gains as he crosses the Male Divide helps him achieve male affirmation he needed as a young teenager at the crossroad of life. Even without the support of a biological father, as he labors to develop the characteristics of a "grown man," a mentor can do what was intended to be accomplished in the home. The positive characteristics he cultivates will bring him true success, even if he lives his entire life without great wealth or remarkable material gain. He will find that the proper measurement of true success is not the size of one's bank account or his collection of "grown-ups toys", but rather it includes things like self-respect, peace of mind, contentment, happiness, the love and admiration of family and friends, the high regard of people in the community and the opportunity to participate in the things that promote the good, wellbeing and success of others. Many so-called successful people in their final days of living are noted as having looked back with irreconcilable regret. They have been known in the final days of their lives, often as life slipped out of their bodies, to express a willingness to trade the whole of their material gains for the love, peace and comfort that comes from meeting the primary needs of the human soul.

The six key characteristics of a "grown man" discussed below contemplate the longings of man's heart. The six qualities are identified in this work as paramount to male success. For instructional purposes there is a natural progression of male affirmation proceeding from the ability to govern, to the ability to discipline, to the ability to sustain, to the ability to protect, to the ability to support, to the ability to nurture. While these are

---

[55] Proverbs 22:1

viewed as progressive steps, genuine growth in one area brings positive change that affects all aspects of a man's life.

The challenges of crossing The Male Divide from the Male Wasteland cannot be overstated. The journey is riddled with difficulties that are often insurmountable for many and proven completely overwhelming for others. Sadly, only a relative few can find in themselves the intestinal fortitude it takes to overcome peer pressures, to handle the perilous hindrances caused by negative people, and to settle the emotional turmoil resulting from the cold, heartless conditions of the wasteland in order to hazard this painful and difficult path. To "Step Up, Step Out" on the passageway that leads to male affirmation presents the greatest challenges most males will ever face, even under the best of circumstances and conditions. But it is especially complicated for those with the unenviable duty of having to traverse this passageway from deep inside the Male Wasteland. And it is even more difficult for individuals living under the darkest conditions like drug addictions, diseases, joblessness, or even incarceration.

This further explains the urgent insistence that the necessary but hazardous "Step Up, Step Out" across the Male Divide cannot be made alone. Truly, it takes a man to affirm another male. Some settings, like a prison environment, are not places most conducive to establishing relationships based on trust such as are necessary to be helpful to an aspiring male-boy. However, before a male-boy can accept the assistance of a mentor, among the first challenges he will face is to overcome the barriers that restrict trust. Fortunately, spiritual fathers who achieved manhood from the Male Wasteland have themselves hazarded this same path and developed the tools needed to help the male-boy take his first critical steps toward affirmation.

The scope of this book will not permit a lengthy discussion of all the qualities listed here. The ability to govern is the most relevant issue to the focus of this work. So, it is discussed at length. Also, since the ability to discipline is the most closely related characteristic to self-governance that step is discussed as well. The other four characteristics, like other related issues mentioned throughout this book, are briefly mentioned and are discussed at length in book to follow this present work.

STEP 1—ABILITY TO GOVERN

The first step out of the Male Wasteland is the ability to govern. Interestingly, since rebellion/lawlessness is the first step down the Slippery Slope leading to the wasteland, self-governance is naturally the starting point for developing the other positive male characteristics. Learning to properly govern one's self is a vital attribute of a responsible adult. The male-boy who chooses rebellion often does so believing he is simply "living his own life" and making decisions based on what he considers are in his best interest. The illusion of rebellion resembles self-governance, but it is not. Like rebellion, self-governance requires personal autonomy, which among other things, calls for independence. It is natural and logical for a boy during the *Choice at the Crossroad* of his life to desire emancipation. In fact, achieving personal freedom to make one's own decisions and seek one's goals is vital to becoming a man.

These tendencies intensify at various stages of human development and reach levels that propel a boy out of the nest into manhood. The changes in the male-boy's attitude and disposition are an indication to his parents and others that the time for male emancipation is approaching. Inasmuch as "doing your own thing" and making one's own decisions feels normal to the male-boy who begins experiencing the new, refreshing sensations associated with adulthood, then the unsuspecting male-boy is often unaware that his rebellious actions are unhealthy. Depending on the skills of his parents, he can also be naive about legitimate ways to achieve the goal of personal independence. Ultimately, if he is unaware and unschooled as to the stage of life he is entering, then the potential for negative rebellion against the "establishment" can become unhealthy with each passing day.

For example, a male-boy might wish to extend his curfew beyond the hour set by his parent(s). After unsuccessfully arguing his point, he may decide to stay out later than expected, despite his parent's insistence to the contrary. He may not realize that as he approaches the age of emancipation the argument with parents is about more than a curfew. Sadly, parents may not recognize this underlined issue either. So, he rebels against the authority over his life and starts down the path that leads to lawlessness. The issue of a restricted curfew becomes the focus of his attention, but the greater matter, which relates to how one enters properly and safely into manhood, is completely overlooked.

A variety of problems lead male-boys into the Male Wasteland, but most often some form of rebellion against an authority figure is involved. Over time, with additional episodes of defiance mixed in, the rebel becomes lawlessness. Men who discuss the history of their failures generally speak in terms of the more noticeable issues that caused them to enter the wasteland. They are surprised to learn that the misstep, during the *Choice at the Crossroad* back when they were teenagers, is also a factor that kept them from developing a mature respect for the "rule of law" as a fundamental life directing concept. The first step across The Male Divide is accepting the role of law as a life principle.

The ability to govern one's self is so primary to being a "grown man" that every other positive trait draws from this capacity. Essentially, this ability involves an understanding that to be independent is not a license to do whatever one pleases, whenever one desires, to whomever one wants, to accomplish a goal however one plans. Imagine a world where no personal restraints exist. A world where no one is required to govern himself in ways that prohibit infringing on the rights of others. Such conditions exist in countries where normal society completely breaks down. Like during the overthrow of some tyrant dictator and the horrible reports that come out of the wickedness, corruption, and malevolence in these countries. It is often so wicked that it is shocking even to the most desensitized ears to hear of how inhumane a human being can be towards another. Lawlessness does not free a society, but rather, handcuffs and reduces its citizens to the lowest denominators of living standards possible.

The obvious truth of this point is so irresistible that readers might be inclined to overlook it in search of a more significant point. But one has only to consider the rise of criminal terrorist activity that displays a total disregard for society; or the insatiable appetites many have for movies and other forms of entertainment that were once considered unacceptable among decent society; or events that depict people living without restraints to realize that our society seems to be trending toward less limitations. Almost anything an individual desire to do these days is considered reasonable, acceptable behavior to some social group or person, even if some unlucky soul or innocent bystander gets hurts in the process. They wrongly conclude that collateral damage cannot be helped and sometimes is a necessary evil justified by the envisioned progress. All such views are wrong and most unfortunate.

At the heart of self-governance is the ability to rule one's self in very definitive and practical way. It is bringing one's thoughts, motives, passions, decision-making processes, and those internal aspects of one's personhood that self-define who he really is under the control of the rule of law. This releases one to be totally free as an individual but with built-in, non-negotiable, proper personal restraints which acknowledge and yields to the rights of others. This "rule of law" must be personal. At its most basic level it is not the law governing society, be it local, state or federal, secular/religious, social or familial that maintains stability. But rather, it is a commitment held by each individual that he must accept personal regulation that makes a society stable. Each person must own lawfulness as a way of life. That acceptance and all it entails for the individual is the rule of law being defined here. It prohibits any form of lawlessness or disregard of the good, established authorities (local, state or federal, secular/religious, social or familial). It views rebellion as abnormal and makes it unacceptable in decent society to be lawless. As one develops the ability to govern, it signals the beginning of the end of negative thinking, positioning him to take this important first "Step Up," and, if he continues the journey "Step Out" of the Male Wasteland.

Practical Application Question:
How does this characteristic apply?

Self-governance impacts a male-boy's ability to function well in traditional male roles. Several remarks are quite telling when made to a male-boy as a type of rebuke or condemnation: "Just suck it up and be a man;" or "When are you going to be a man?" or "Are you a man or a boy?!" or "Just be a man about it!" or "I thought you said you were a man." There is an unspoken understanding of what a man is or is not and a general expectation about what is expected of one functioning in a man's role.

Certain "codes" are considered as normal characteristics of a "grown man." These codes are considered a badge of honor and like the uniform of a solider or a metal one earns for heroic feats done in battle are worn and displayed proudly. The codes of a "grown man" distinguish and separate him from all others. An affirmed man who has successfully crossed the Male Divide is known for having specific qualities, including the following three codes: a code of vows, a code of strength, and a code of honor.

Code of Vows

"A man's word is his bond." There is hardly a male-boy who has not had this phrase uttered to him as a means of communicating the importance of keeping his promises and commitments through to completion. It is such an established expectation that being a man requires one to keep true to his word that if one fails to do what he said he would he is hardly taken seriously and is viewed as an immature person. What's more, the broad usage of contracts in today's world is in itself a reminder of declining values in our society. In years past what was once accomplished with a firm handshake as two men looked eye to eye, now requires an attorney who is skilled in the use of precise language. He is needed to write the contract in an unambiguous way so that a client's own words are not used against him; and also, to read a contract to ensure that his client does not commit in ways that disadvantages him.

Why an attorney? Because traits like personal integrity, truthfulness, and fair play often take a back seat to greed, the lust for power, material gain and the like. Many couples make marriage vows with the understanding that if the relationship does not work out (whatever that means), then the marriage will be politely ended, freeing each person to pursue another relationship. The traditional popular statement that all couples once recited during the wedding ceremony, "Until death we part" is no longer a part of the ceremony or thought process.

In other contracts, some individuals secretly put words in the fine print of the details to gain an advantage over the other party in some tricky way. It is getting increasingly difficult to accept another person's word at face value. People rarely say what they really mean, which puts the listener in a "wait and see" position in reference to a person's word. So, "I'll believe it, when I see it" is the sarcastic remark made so often by a disappointed person whose trust has been violated so often that he has completely lost confidence in the "spoken word." You have probably heard the well-intended advice, "Believe only half of what you hear a person say and all of what you see him do," and, "I'd rather see a sermon than to hear one any day."

These statements highlight the fact that our society has become more cynical as people become less and less trustworthy about their word.

Traditionally, this would be referred to as being untruthful or lying. But in many cultural circles today it has a much less condemning connotation. In fact, it might be viewed as impolite to label one as a liar, since he is simply doing what is required to protect himself and others. But over time such a practice begins to characterize and define the individual who habitually misrepresents the truth.

Unfortunately, for male-boys on the Slippery Slope, lying is often a way of life. Many of them start being less than honest during the early stages of rebellion, before lawlessness takes root. In far too many situations, telling someone how you truly feel or disclosing too much of your thoughts can give a disingenuous person an unfair or unreasonable advantage over you. This provides another layer of faulty reasoning for the male-boy, causing him to decide incorrectly that it is safer even better to hide behind half-truths and lies as a means of avoiding as many conflicts as possible. This is preferred over confronting people face to face or dealing with unpleasant situations directly.

As he moves down the Slippery Slope, dishonesty becomes a way of life for him. Consequently, the value of his words loses meaning and after a while he destroys the natural tendency a person has to keep his words sacred. He becomes so untrustworthy that everything he says is suspect. It has been correctly said that "a man is only as good as his word." As a result, a male-boy's failure to keep his word can turn out to be such a sore spot in his relationships that it contributes to the decline and destruction of every human bond he holds dear.

Directly connected with this truth vacuum is how common it is in the Male Wasteland for male-boys to avoid making any promises whatsoever. It is an attempt to keep from dishonoring their word and not misrepresent themselves. On the surface this might seem honorable, since it is preferable for a person to not make a promise rather than fail to keep it. One problem with this position, however, is that it stifles and can destroy the opportunity for a person to have high-quality interpersonal relations.

Perhaps it is noteworthy that some of the same individuals who are not unwilling to give their word and stand on it might not hesitate to sign a loan contract or to make a verbal pledge of intent to repay a favor if doing so advances their selfish purposes. Making a vow, a promise, a pledge is a prerequisite for forming healthy human relationships. One who refuses to make promises or to clearly express his intention to conduct himself in a trustworthy manner is most likely unwilling to live in open relationship with others.

Self-governance is demonstrated on a basic level in how well one masters his own words. Since the ability to govern must be established in the individual as a life pattern before he can be effective in this area, one learns to value his words by maintaining control over his tongue. The tendency to speak, or agree, or promise before one hears all the facts or carefully considers the matter is often linked to why a person promises more than he should. If one over promises, he will invariably under deliver. Too many male-boys engage in a great deal of idle conversations about insignificant, even worthless matters, talking before thinking. Controlling one's tongue is a personal discipline achieved partly by talking less and listening more.[56] The ability to govern is an important way to minimize this tendency.

Code of Strength

Weakness is not an option for a "grown man." He must have "iron in his blood." It is imperative that he have a firmness about him and a stability in his character and emotions that demonstrates his ability to defend his proper self-interest. A man must be able to protect his need to find his voice and to defend his right to express his thoughts and opinions. He must do each of these while standing solidly on the decisions he makes. Nothing is more intolerable in any social structure than a male-boy

---

[56] James 1:19; James 3:1-10

trying to operate in a "grown man's" role, without the strong constitution of a man.

Another less obvious consequence of using lies for self-protection is how that moral deficiency contributes to the male-boy becoming a coward. He lacks the ability to look another man "eye to eye" with an inherent confidence that comes from knowing he is formidable in his own right and up to any challenge seeking to deny his rightful stance. He cowers on every front refusing even to express his thoughts or ideas about matters that impact his life directly. Unable to protect himself, he most certainly is unable to stand up for his family. Such a male-boy cannot command the common respect a man is due and must live beneath his privilege in society.

The challenges in life that mount against an individual with positive goals are direct, pressing, consistent and unavoidable. This is true generally, but it is especially noticed when one is attempting to regain positions he has lost or forfeited through bad choices. Making a comeback against seemingly insurmountable odds, such as those found in the Male Wasteland, present the most difficult challenges a male-boy will likely ever face. He must find the "heart" the guts and grit it will take to maintain positive goals. This is the character strength he needs to "be his own man" and not permit peer pressure or "group think" to rearrange his priorities or dictate his actions.

But this strength is also needed to rise above disappointments, setbacks and the personal failures one may face on his journey. Strength of mind, willpower and determination are among the mental, emotional tools needed to confront big challenges and refuse to quit. The male-boy who gives up on legitimate responsibilities and duties is weak mentally, emotionally and or spiritually, even if he can bench-press 400 pounds of dead weight. It takes a "grown man" to stay the course against forces stronger than he, or to face obstacles that cannot be moved but must be overcome. Quitting is often the easier course, but it is also a dream killer.

For the "grown man" quitting is not a practicable option. Instead, he makes a habit out of rising and "getting back in the game." He sees the task at hand all the way through to the end or until there is absolutely no other working alternative available. Only the actions of others and restraints outside his control that make it impossible for him to complete a task slow his progress. But even then the "grown man" realigns his approach, reassesses his options, searches for an alternative plan and finds the best way to achieve the goal another way. He does not easily take "no" for an answer or look for the easy way out as a first solution to overcoming a hazard in his path. He is unwilling to accept the path of least resistance if by doing so he must abandon his goals and dreams. He sees himself as formidable to the challenges he faces.

It takes a strong man to maintain this type of dogged determination that refuses to give in to forces working against him. With this strength he brings meaning to his faith and can say without fear: *"I can do all things through Christ who strengthens me;"*[57] *"If God be for us (me) who can be against us (me);"*[58] *"In all these things we are (I am) more than conquerors through Christ who loves us (me);"*[59] *"No weapons formed against me shall be able to prosper;"*[60] *"With men it is impossible but with God all things are possible;"*[61] and, *"If you (I) can believe, all things are possible to him that believes."* [62]

Code of Honor

There was a time in American society where certain niceties were common. Do you remember when *chivalry* (which is gallantry, courtliness, politeness, courtesy, graciousness, good manners, etc.) was a

---

[57] Philippians 4:13
[58] Romans 8:31
[59] Romans 8:37
[60] Isaiah 54:17
[61] Matthew 19:26
[62] Mark 9:23

common male characteristic in this society? When men tipped their hats to women as they passed by on the walk, or opened a woman's door, or stepped aside to permit her to pass, or pulled her chair at the table, or did not discuss certain issues and subjects in mixed company of women and

children? If any of this sounds strange, then that makes the point. Of course, thankfully in some circles, chivalry is not dead. But it is rapidly fading in our modern world.

But what does chivalry have to do with the ability to govern? Primarily, personal governance is a social issue. This begins to explain why throughout this document the writer repeatedly refers to an individual's responsibilities to "decent society." While there are obvious personal advantages associated with self-governance, other members of society also benefit. Some profit directly and others more indirectly from a male-boy who achieves this characteristic, but the best interests of a society are served by individuals who govern themselves well.

Furthermore, self-governance is a fundamental prerequisite of respect. The male-boy who lacks the ability to govern himself is rarely inclined to respect others. Much of the insensitivities many males have for their female counterparts are due to an absence of basic human regard and respect for the being and rights of others.

A "grown man" governs himself in ways that safeguard against disrespecting others. Of course, the traditional male role in society call for a man to possess other characteristics. Nurturing and protecting for example especially highlights the need for a man to respect women and children in decent society. The extent to which a man cultivates the ability to govern himself determines his ability to develop the capacity for respecting others and position himself properly to fulfill the other important male roles.

1. *How does this characteristic relate to God, self, family and society?*

How it relates to God

A man with the ability to govern himself:

- recognizes the obligation to remain loyal to God's sovereign authority as the Creator and only Ruler worthy of Lordship; avoiding the tendency to make himself a "god"

- makes all of his vows in the name of the Almighty God to whom he holds himself accountable for keeping his word

- seeks and relies on God as the only source from which he achieves the personal intestinal fortitude (staying power, grit, guts, courage, stamina, determination) required of a man

How it relates to self

A man with the ability to govern himself:

- maintains a healthy self-love and self-respect that manifest in his ability to properly meet his own needs

- holds his word and promises as essential aspects of his personal integrity

- obligates himself to keep with the highest integrity every commitment he makes; confronting all obstacles; facing every challenge; and working to overcome any difficulties so that failing to complete the task, reach the goal or quitting is not an option no matter the circumstances

How it relates to family

A man with the ability to govern himself:
- is able to correctly govern his family based on love, integrity and mutual respect
- keeps the promises he makes to his family as a sacred trust and duty in which he delights and he prioritizes his commitments to them above every other earthly pursuit under God

- conducts himself in a manner that provides his family with a strong, reliable shoulder to lean on that:

  ✓ does not waver under the burden of his responsibilities;

  ✓ will not lose heart in the heat of battling obstacles;

  ✓ refuses to give in to the pressures or normal stresses associated with meeting his obligations;

  ✓ and is unwilling to quit no matter the problem

How it relates to society

A man with the ability to govern himself:

- disavows and refuses allegiances with others that would compromise himself to God, self or family; accepts as personally binding the good, established laws governing society, whether local, state or federal, secular/religious, social or familial

- holds as a matter of personal integrity the responsibility to fulfill pledges he makes as a citizen and participant in civic, religious and social institutions
- helps to encourage other citizens to maintain his integrity, to remain loyal to societal goals, and to work untiringly for the good of citizens and institutions

2. *What is required to develop the ability to govern?*

A. Carefully evaluate the positive benefits of self-governance and the negative consequences one experiences by improper self-governance

B. Make a firm, irreversible decision and commitment to be a self-governing person

C. Admit that rebellion and lawlessness have failed as a way of life

D. Acknowledge one's determination to develop the ability to govern one's self

E. Admit one's need to be accountable to a mentor(s)

F. Swallow your pride and establish accountability with a mentor(s)

G. Discuss and disclose one's specific issues of lawlessness with a mentor(s)

H. Begin keeping every rule applicable to one's situations in life without having to be told or reminded to do so by others

I. Govern one's self in every small thing required whether you like it or not, or whether you agree with it or not

J. Refuse to break rules for any reason even if it makes you uncomfortable, if it is inconvenient, or if it creates tensions between you and others

K. Pay special attention to the promises one makes; be conscientious about doing what you say; stop refusing to make promises to avoid having to be a man of your word; make commitments as one should, put one's word on it and keep it

L. Refuse to give up, give in or give out; do not quit no matter the difficulty of the challenge or how imposing the hindrance may be; stand firm and refuse to be swayed; be fully determined to do all that is required of you to maintain your commitments

M. Respect others—their rights, their person, their space; their needs; be mindful of your obligations to honor others, especially women and children

STEP 2—ABILITY TO DISCIPLINE

The second step leading out of the Male Wasteland is the ability to discipline. Self-discipline is the control one has over himself through which he molds, perfects and corrects his mental faculties, physical abilities and moral character in prescribed ways that result in a well-ordered and regulated lifestyle. A "grown man" exercises control over his thoughts, attitudes, passions, words and actions. His disciplines flow from inside his soul and spirit and are manifested in all that he says and does. He has a concept of "self" that is not determined by others around him in society or within his peer group.

This definition highlights the importance once again of self-governance and why it must precede discipline. A lawless person is so self-centered and selfish that he lacks the willingness to engage in activities with the purpose of encouraging order. Because an unruly person is by definition disobedient, unmanageable, disruptive and wild, he lives without regulation. Further, he is often actually supported in his rebellious and bad behaviors by others around him. There will always be people who do not desire the change and growth of the person wanting to climb out of the Male Wasteland. They will put all sorts of peer pressures upon him to *not* change his ways or leave their group. The personal disciplines required to reject the beliefs, influences, and inducements of these blocking persons are not often possible for a young male who does not have any real sense of "self" and who does not self-govern properly.

For a person to abandon lifelong friends, give up long-held social affiliations with organizations and gangs, and even redefine family relationships that are centered in questionable lifestyles, demands disciplines that can only be developed within an individual who has the courage and learned ability to self-govern. Accordingly, the first step out of the Male Wasteland (the ability to self-govern and to get beyond being so largely- concerned about what the gang peer group or his social environment demands) must be fully achieved, at least attitudinally, before this second step of ability to discipline self can be realized.

Personal disciplines are not somehow separate from an individual's everyday lifestyle, nor are personal disciplines stagnating when produced well. In fact, the failure to connect disciplines in natural ways to one's life likely accounts for why some individuals find extra difficulties when attempting to shape a new discipline into a normal part of who the person is and what he does. Discipline as a way of life comes across as "real" not fake or phony. The perceptions that others have about the disciplined person tend to be more favorable toward that individual. Furthermore, the individual who builds a personal discipline carefully will likely reap the valuable and helpful emotional benefits that come from hard work and a sense of accomplishment.

It is important to emphasize the overall role of discipline in a male-boy's life even before the discussion of the specific disciplines one must have to "Step Up, Step Out" the Male Wasteland. Perhaps it is helpful here to breakdown the definition for self-discipline given above. This definition will clarify the general role of discipline as a lifestyle and how it is applicable to each discipline one must develop.

"Self-discipline is the control one has over himself through which he molds, perfects and corrects his mental faculties and physical abilities in prescribed ways that result in a well-ordered and regulated lifestyle":

- ***Self-discipline is the control one has over himself***

Control is the essential element of self-discipline. The male-boy determined to self-govern must learn to manage himself so he can exercise power over his thinking and behavioral patterns in order to bring his emotions and deeds under control. There are relationships and things in his life that he must manage and control. To function well in these capacities, he must have command of himself. A male-boy should first make the commitment to the necessity of "control" before he begins the demanding sometimes difficult task involved in developing a discipline.

• *He molds, perfects and corrects*

The work of developing a personal discipline is hard work and should be approached with the attitude that "if it is worth doing, it is worth doing well." In some instances, this can call for a kind of personal makeover, challenging a person to rethink, even redefine himself. *Correcting* and *perfecting* oneself is the language of *change*. There is a natural resistance to change when patterns have been firmly established; especially the type of changes that are related to developing personal disciplines. Making this type of change will force a person to not only address old habits and patterns of thinking and behaving, but he must reevaluate beliefs, even adjust core values. Change at this level is hard work. A male-boy should make a firm commitment to do all that is necessary to reshape himself and reach the ideal person envisioned by the discipline he seeks to form.

• *Mental faculties and physical abilities*

Personal disciplines involve concrete aspects of an individual's being. Avoiding superficial change requires growth that affects the way one gathers, processes and uses information and includes how one reasons, filters emotions and draws conclusions. Since some physical conditioning is generally involved in developing a discipline, even if it is mostly mental (like meditation), physical conditioning is also an important part of personal discipline. The male-boy must intentionally and deliberately engage body, mind, and spirit in forming disciplines so that his growth is holistic, natural, and unyielding. In doing so he positions himself to make permanent personal adjustments.

- ***In prescribed ways that result in a well- ordered and regulated lifestyle***

Developing a personal discipline requires precise activity that directs growth meticulously toward a determined end. Ultimately personal disciplines are the building blocks of moral character. A regulated lifestyle helps an individual keep pace with all the vital aspects of his life and other areas of commitments he has, so he can maintain every role in good working harmony. Every discipline has a prescribed set of functions that make demands on an individual to follow certain patterns. Over time the habit-forming patterns can become like second nature to the individual that are reflected in normal natural ways.

Practical Application Question:
How does this characteristic apply?

But what are the personal disciplines a "grown man" has that distinguish him from a male boy and position him to function in a man's roles? The short list of personal disciplines a male-boy should develop includes a *positive attitude,* a *healthy body,* a *temperate personality,* a *faithful nature,* a *strong work ethic,* and a *cooperative, teachable spirit.* This list is not intended to be comprehensive, but it includes six of the disciplines evident in a "grown man" that contributes to the successes he experiences in every male role he assumes. Whether one is evaluating the successful son, brother, husband, father, entrepreneur, worker, citizen, volunteer, mentor or friend these six disciplines are measureable qualities present in that man. Conversely, when these specific personal disciplines are absence or significantly lacking in a male-boy, it can account for the strained and failed relationships that impede his ability to achieve success in the areas those relationships represent. Failed relationships are directly attributable to weak or missing personal disciplines.

Acquiring a personal discipline is difficult. It is achieved through an often-long state and series of painful preparations. Circumstances will offer many reasons to give up and quit. The serious-minded person must observe a strict regimen involving things he may not like or know how to do. There will be setbacks and drawbacks. Developing a discipline may pull him away from comfort zones; or he may become the source of jest, or worse, ridicule. But if he is determined to succeed, he must find the intestinal fortitude to see it through, despite the discomforts or inconveniences.

While the arranged order of the personal disciplines listed below is unimportant, an aspiring male attempting to successfully cross the Male Divide must achieve a level of competence in each of these six areas. These personal disciplines once mastered have a synergetic effect in the individual increasing his ability to regulate relationships. One of the outcomes of this empowering energy is in how the affirmed male develops an internal structure for channeling and directing his gifts, talents and other personal assets. It positions him to face challenges and overcome the negative influences and forces in the Male Wasteland that work against success. Since these disciplines are not progressive steps, but the combined action of each working together gives the individual the greater capabilities required to "Step Up, Step Out" the Male Wasteland, then simultaneous, diligent effort to develop each discipline can and should be applied.

Discipline #1—Positive Attitude

An attitude is a mental position one develops naturally in relations to the people, things and circumstances he encounters directly or indirectly. This description is somewhat contrary to the common thinking which suggests that people develop attitudes in a kind of thought-filled decision-making process as one weighs the pros and cons of life's situations. Quite to the contrary, the definition above makes clear that <u>a person cannot "not" form an attitude (a mental position) in reference to the people and situations he encounters through his life experiences</u>. An individual can decide how an attitude impacts the course of his life. Indeed, whether he wins or loses with the attitudes he has is a matter of choice. Since most people will agree that winning is preferable to losing, it is reasonable for us to work toward developing positive attitudes positions that help us reach constructive goals and achieve success.

But maintaining a positive attitude must be a deliberate act, it must be done "on purpose," and it requires discipline. The male-boy must train and condition himself to think positively. It may escape his awareness that "thinking" is one of the things he must make an enormous investment if he wants to succeed. Thinking is a basic human function that everyone does more than anything else, but it is strange how little training we receive or preparation we make for how we process and use information. Everyone thinks all the time, but thinking *well* is an art that does not come easy and can only be achieved by those willing to put in the work it takes to do it right.

Since attitudes form naturally, the goal for acquiring a discipline in this area involves attaining critical thinking skills. Several basic steps contribute to thinking clearly, including *considering the source of information, allowing for different viewpoints, questioning the opinions and assumptions of the one(s) with whom the information originated, weighing the background and circumstances of the information, identifying any false reasoning or prejudices,* and *comparing and/or contrasting your conclusions with your own values.* Realizing these steps calls for developing several key skills. These steps are not intended to be all-inclusive, but the list does contain some of the crucial skills involved in critical thinking, including:

1. The ability to properly observe in order to gather the "real" information
2. The ability to grasp meaning and interpret facts accurately
3. The ability to use information, concepts, and theories to solve problems
4. The ability to see patterns in order to make out deeper meanings
5. The ability to draw conclusions that are in line with facts and intended meaning
6. The ability to recognize subjectivity

A positive attitude requires a mind that is <u>settled,</u> <u>focused</u> and <u>sober.</u> A **settled mind** is still, quiet, not busy. It is a mind that has been brought to rest, removed and relieved from distress. The collection of life issues to think about, the situations with which to deal, and the problems—some resolved, some unresolved—pile up day by day in the human mind and cause an enormous amount of internal noise.

To combat the mental, emotional disturbance this noise causes, the male-boy builds distractions into his daily routines in an attempt to quiet the clatter and racket in his mind. But his daily practices often contribute to his lack of discipline and can include things (some of which are good and innocent) that supply the very dysfunctions he needs to confront and overcome.

The male-boy's habits that hinder the development of disciplines are evident in the amount of time he spends in *entertainment* activities (television, movies, sports, video games, recreation, music devices, etc.), in the amount of *time he spends asleep* and in *leisure*, in the investments he puts into *drugs, alcohol* and other substances, and in some cases even in the energy he puts into *work* and other legitimate activities. Any of these can become subtle hindrances for maintaining a settled mind.

Discipline #2-A Focused Mind

A **focused mind** is alert, not distracted or careless. It pays attention; it listens carefully; it is all ears; it is on the ball, and it is ready to act. At the center of this mindset is a clear focal point, the heart of individual thought, which spotlights the things that are of primary importance. The unfocused male-boy does not see the warning signs signaling dangers in his path; nor does he hear the alarms that sound off like the sirens of emergency vehicles, alerting other travelers on the road ahead of the need to move aside so as to not impede its progress.

Many excellent opportunities and emerging obstacles are missed by the untrained male-boy who is not conscious of his surroundings. By learning to focus his mind on properly set goals, the male-boy can avoid the distractions that cause one to neglect the weightier matters of life in favor of frivolous and temporary pleasures that cannot make a solid foundation upon which to build a successful future. This is the aspect of a disciplined mind that helps the male-boy to "fix his thoughts on the things that are above, not upon those that are on earth."[63] He can now "seek first God's Kingdom and the righteousness it requires, and then all these things he needs including food, shelter and clothing will be acquired."[64]

Discipline #3- A Sober Mind

A **sober mind** is clear-headed, serious, constrained, and not thoughtless. It is realistic, down-to-earth, cool, calm and collected. Picture someone with an earnestly thoughtful demeanor who is rational and

---

[63] Colossians 3:2
[64] Matthew 6:33

reasonable in his responses to people, circumstances and things and you are doubtless looking at a sober minded person. The sober minded person avoids the tendency to react. In tense moments and stressful situations, he pushes the pause button, counts to ten, and when necessary takes a deep breath before he speaks or acts.

The male-boy is often overemotional and uncontained dealing with difficult situations and people. This largely accounts for why he can be viewed by others has being unstable; and why he may become defensive, rude and flippant when he gets into situations where he is in over his head.

He comes across as immature and light-minded, because he does not have the disciplines required to give measured, well-conceived responses when presented with hard questions, nor does he possess the skills useful for responding to challenging situations in thoughtful ways. He may in fact know what to do in or about the situation; he may have answers to any questions being asked; or he may have a solution to a problem he is encountering. But without a sober mind he will have a weakened response.

Another way of considering the idea of being sober is in reference to abstaining from the abusive use of alcohol or drugs. A "drunkard" or "druggy" is not sober. Such a person loses his capacity for self-restraint. His thought processes are not sensible and in many instances simply crazy.

Some people might argue that the male-boy probably causes more interference for himself and compromises his own future more under the influence of some substance than at any other time. This certainly happens quite often. However, failure to develop the type of no-nonsense thinking such as a sober minded person has is perhaps counterproductive in ways that negatively impacts all of the male-boy's relationships.

These three aspects of a functional mind—*settled, focused and sober*—have traits that are vital for cultivating the critical thinking skills listed above. Among the spiritual gifts that God gives to those who are determined to live the Christ-life is that he keeps us from a "spirit of fear" and gives us a spirit "of power, and of love, and of a sound mind."[65]

A sound mind is largely a part of the by-products of the commitment to godliness. It takes a disciplined mind to process, analyze, use and store information in ways that can enable an individual to think clearly and critically. The doctrine of renewing the mind is an important teaching found throughout the Bible and is central to Christian theology.

---

[65] 2 Timothy 1:7

STANDARDS FOR EFFECTIVE/EFFICIENT LEADERSHIP FUNCTIONS (SEELF)

Facilitator Guide

STANDARDS FOR EFFECTIVE/EFFICIENT LEADERSHIP FUNCTIONS (SEELF) is designed to provide theoretical information and practical skills training to help mentors become effective and efficient leaders. Peer leadership is effective when competency standards established for evaluation are met and are efficient as they demonstrate the ability to use resources proficiently.

I: PRACTICAL DEFINITIONS

Definitions can either be theoretical or practical. Theoretical definitions usually offer a general viewpoint of a word, relying on abstract principles and speculation. Practical definitions give information that goes beyond theory or ideal; it is useful information that is action oriented and capable of being put to use. Practical definitions are used throughout this series to highlight the action associated with the terms defined. This is especially helpful when discussing leadership roles. The definition of the term discloses the action associated with the leadership role.

A. **Leader**—one whose ideas, strength, and courageous acts guide others on the way and directs their behavior in a manner that causes them to follow.

B. **Leadership**—influence of a group of leaders who work in concert with each other to initiate and activate change and direct the movement of their group towards clearly defined goals. Three primary leadership objectives:

1. How to delegate
2. How to motivate
3. How to regulate
   a. One's self
   b. Others

C. **Effective**—having and using the ability and power to accomplish actual purpose and intent.

D. **Efficient**—properly and adequately using all available resources in the most useful and least wasteful manner possible to achieve an intended purpose.

CRITICAL THINKING QUESTIONS:

1. Do you presently consider yourself a leader by the above definitions, or at least some other definition of your own? Why or why not? What alternate definitions do you have for what makes a leader?

_____

_____

_____

2. What do the words "ideas", "strength" and "courageous acts" in the above definition for a leader mean to you?

_____

_____

_____

3. If you are a leader, can you work effectively and efficiently with other leaders? What would work within a leadership structure mean to you?

_____

_____

_____

_____

_____

4. Can there feasibly be many leaders working together? How? What would each leader need to do to function effectively and efficiently with the others for achievement of their overall leadership goals?

_____

_____

_____

_____

_____

II: DEFINING PEER-LEADERSHIP

There are three primary roles in the leadership model. Generally, an individual does not function effectively in each role with the same person. These specific roles and functions, while defined broadly below, must take on a functional meaning for effectiveness in a prison environment.

A. Mentor

One who is a close, trusted, and experienced guide who can hold up a mirror for another, who can help motivate decisions, and who is committed to helping the mentored achieve his goals by being a:

1. *Friend*—one who seeks the society or welfare of another whom he holds in affection, respect, or esteem, or whose companionship and personality are pleasurable

2. *Tutor*—one who is charged with the instruction and guidance of another

3. *Coach*—one who trains intensively by detailed instruction, frequent demonstration and repeated practice

An effective mentor has to operate on some level in all three of these capacities (friend, tutor, coach) to gain the proper respect of those he serves.

B. Facilitator—one that helps to bring about an outcome (as learning, productivity, or communication) by providing indirect or unobtrusive assistance, guidance, or supervision

C. Teacher—one who causes knowledge and skills by accustoming another to some action or attitude through instruction, training, and discipline

CRITICAL THINKING QUESTIONS:

1. Which role is more important? More effective? —to be a friend, a tutor, or a coach, to a mentored person? Why?

_____

_____

_____

_____

2. Which role is more important? More effective? ---to be a facilitator, or a teacher, to a mentored person? Why?

_____

_____

_____

_____

3. Which of the above-described mentoring levels or capacities best suit your personal nature and style? Why?

_____

_____

_____

_____

_____

4. Can you, as a leader and mentor, operate on levels that perhaps you have not tried before or that are not in your comfort zone?

_____

_____

_____

_____

III: *GENERAL LEADERSHIP REQUIREMENTS*

Functioning effectively in any peer leadership role requires personal inventory to call attention to any personal attitude, belief, practice, or position one may have that could negatively impact one's ability to lead another.

As outlined below, a leader should have *personal awareness* of what predispositions, assumptions, or perceptions he might be laboring-under; coupled with *personal disciplines* so as to not permit those to interfere with his leadership potential; and be able to accept and handle and not misuse the privileges and challenges of his *power position.*

Personal Awareness

1. Predispositions—values/beliefs one has that affect the way he receives, accepts, interacts, or relates with another

2. Assumptions—one's supposition that something is true, factual and is likely taken for granted

3. Perceptions—a formed mental position/image interpreted in light of one's collective personal experiences

Every leader needs as a starter to be aware that he, like all human beings, will have inevitably been shaped and influenced by his upbringing, background, and learned attitudes, beliefs, practices, and positions. These go as far back as his childhood, how he was raised, his home and social and cultural milieu as he grew up, the things that happened to him at impressionable moments in his life. We are all a product of our environments. In *Breaking Barriers,* author and teacher Gordon Graham discusses how each of us see the world around us through a window of our own acquired beliefs and views, and how we need to change the things "written on our window", in order for us to stop being influenced by those perceptions of reality.

For the leader, it is particularly-important that he be self-aware of how he may be perceiving or viewing things and those whom he presumes to lead. He must guard against *predispositions*, assumptions, and *perceptions* about others, so he does not unwittingly fall prey to his own prejudices or attitudes he may be fostering within himself. He must guard against his leadership being shaped by what he might incorrectly or prejudicially believe or think, and *personal awareness* and self-inventory should be the first step.

B. Personal Disciplines

1. Modeling the change you want others to adopt—lead and guide by one's own personal example

2. Exemplifying self-control and self-discipline—show consistent and principled leadership, with responsible, temperate, and well-modulated responses to the stresses and challenges of leadership

3. Maintaining positive lifestyle and good personal conduct—demonstrating self-respect, integrity, and responsibility in every aspect of one's own life and behavior and attitude

A leader must have his own house in order before he presumes to lead or guide others in how they should run theirs. He must be a model to those he works with and serves, using his own self-example daily to show them the better way. A leader must exemplify excellent attributes of self-control and self-discipline, to not fall prey to prejudice or preconceptions about others; to demonstrate well-mannered, just, and proper leadership; and to show by his own life and actions what others should aspire to.

C. Power Positions

1. Privileges of the position—rights, benefits, rank, authority, prestige, recognition, respect

2. Challenges of the position—needing to lead by example, being under constant scrutiny, being accountable, "never off the clock", stress, exhaustion, facing opposition and criticism

3. Responsibilities of the position—modeling, mediating, mentoring, making tough decisions, being wise and judicious, balancing firmness with fairness

A leader must be always mindful that with his power position comes not just the privileges of leadership and authority, but also the responsibilities and challenges of that. He must be highly principled about never misusing his rank and authority for his own personal goals or self-gratification. He must be above reproach in his personal conduct and behavior and attitude. He must accept the difficulties and unpleasant aspects of being a leader, along with its benefits and perks. He must constantly be worthy of and earn whatever respect or esteem he is held in by those he leads.

CRITICAL THINKING QUESTIONS:

1. *What, if any, is the correlation between personal awareness, personal disciplines, and personal positions?*

_____

_____

_____

_____

_____

2. *What are the rewards of a working sensitivity to these three requirements?*

_____

_____

_____

_____

_____

3. *As explained in the team concept of H.E.A.R.T, describe the relevance of the value "accountability" in relationship to the other values.*

_____

_____

_____

_____

4. *What important personal factors should you consider when deciding to make adjustments to predispositions you have in order to improve relations with others?*

_____

_____

_____

_____

_____

5. *What argument would you present to convince another that the personal development required to perfect these sensitivities is beneficial to him specifically and the community generally?*

_____

_____

_____

_____

_____

_____

IV: ROLES

A role is a function performed by someone in a particular situation, operation or process, with a set of clearly defined standards governing the conduct of the person in that position. Every role includes three aspects leaders must consider and perfect to function effectively, including *expectations, performance and conflict.*

A. Role-Expectation

Role-expectation is related to what is expected from an individual's position and how that role *should be* carried out and viewed by others. There are *Five Expectation Standards* required for any role. Every expectation should be measured and evaluated based on these five standards. Any expectation that is not reasonable, just, proper, due or necessary should be challenged and perhaps rejected.

The Five Expectation Standards:

1. **Reasonable** (moderate, well-tempered—not extreme or excessive)
2. **Just** (correct, conforming with what is morally upright or good)
3. **proper** (limited to the specified idea),
4. **due** (rightfully owed; obligation required)
5. **necessary** (logically unavoidable; cannot be denied without contradiction)

There are two types of expectations:

Type One Expectations—What do you expect of yourself?

In the space provided list your personal goals and responsibilities that require expectations of you? Measure each item you list by the *Five Expectation Standards* list. Determine if each expectation you list is reasonable, just, proper, due, and necessary.

<u>Type Two Expectations—What do people expect of leaders?</u>
1. **Integrity** (honest, sound and principled (incorruptible))
2. **Trustworthy** (worthy of confidence; dependable)
3. **Respectful** (considering others worthy of high regard; esteeming others)
4. **Loyal** (unswerving allegiance to others; faithful to the cause, ideal, custom)
5. **Active** (fully engaged, energetic and action-oriented)
6. **Knowledgeable** (having an experiential familiarity and understanding about the program and the solution to problems)

B. Role-Performance

Role-performance is related to how a role is *actually* being performed (despite how it should be performed), which may or may not align with either a person's self-imposed expectations or the expectations others have of him.

1) Performance objectives should include—specific information defining the role from broad perspectives including:

   a. What the role involves (specific duties, scheduling issues, reports, personal sacrifices, etc.)

   b. Timelines

   c. Performance measures and methods

2) Evaluation of one's personal ability to perform:

   a. How to get the most out of one's strengths?

   b. How to improve one's weaknesses

c. How to determine the limits of one's ability?

C. Role-Conflict

Role conflict is unavoidable because each person has more than one important role with many responsibilities competing for his time, attention and resources. Finding the balance with every role one has is an ongoing responsibility that must never be neglected, because role conflict can create tensions that makes one ineffective in every role. There are several keys to minimizing conflicts:

1) Prioritize personal goals responsibly. Effective prioritizing must recognize that everything cannot be first; something has to be second, third, etc.
Step 1: Prioritize within each goal
Step 2: Prioritize goal to goal and establish one's priority list

2) Manage joint-responsibilities that impact role performance.
   a. Identify the functions of others that directly connect to your performance
   b. Reach clear agreements with others concerning who does what when and how

3) Address conflicts as soon as possible; delayed responses to issues serve to worsen problems.

CRITICAL THINKING QUESTIONS:

1. *What is your present role, and what do people expect of you in that? Is your view of yourself and how you are viewed by others a reasonable, just, proper, due, and necessary role expectation?*

_____

_____

_____

_____

expectation of leaders (integrity, trustworthiness, respectfulness, loyalty, activeness, and knowledgeableness) that others have of them is most important that they fulfill? Why?

_____

_____

_____

_____

2. *What aspect of role do you struggle with: role-expectation, role-performance, or role conflict? How, and why?*

_____

_____

_____

_____

3. *Discuss one experience you had when one role that you have conflicted with another? How did you deal with that?*

_____

_____

_____

_____

_____

_____

_____

_____

V: SKILLS/COMPETENCY

A *skill* is the ability to use one's knowledge effectively and readily in execution or performance of a task. *Competency* is having the required or adequate ability, qualities or capacity to function or develop in a particular way. Knowing about a skill, that it is, what it is, or even how and why it is, is not having the ability to put the skill into practice nor reaching a point of competency in the skill. In their book, *Looking Out, Looking In*, authors Ronald Adler and Neil Towne identify four stages in learning skills:

- Stage 1—*Beginning Awareness* (Learn that there is a new and better way of behaving)

- Stage 2—*Awkward* (Initial attempts at using the new skill)

- Stage 3—*Consciously Skilled* (Become comfortable with using the new skill well)

- Stage 4—*Integrated* (Able to perform the skill without thinking about it)

Knowing these stages is helpful because one can prepare himself to work through the startup difficulties of learning a new skill. The determination to master a skill encourages one to make the personal investments that create success. When the skill is developed, the sacrifice and work involved in mastering it will be well worth the effort.

Seven easy steps are identified for learning new skills:
- ✓ Complete the pre/post evaluation
- ✓ Introduce the skill (discuss the specific and concrete behaviors involved in the skill)
- ✓ Model the skill (practice the skill with a role-play exercise(s))
- ✓ Discuss broader usages of the skill
- ✓ Experiment with the skill
- ✓ Adapt the skill personally
- ✓ Complete the pre/post evaluation

CRITICAL THINKING QUESTIONS:

1. *What is a leadership or mentoring skill that you would like to have? What is your present stage (as discussed above) in learning or developing that skill?*

_____

_____

_____

_____

_____

2. *What is a skill that you have that you could lend to leadership or that you could teach someone else so they could lead and mentor with it, too?*

_____

_____

_____

_____

3. *What skills or lack of skills do you see, right now, with leadership in place? How would you change or improve those?*

_____

_____

_____

_____

4. *What do YOU offer skill-wise as a leader and mentor? What can you bring to the table?*

_____

_____

_____

_____

SOCIAL SKILLS

Social Skills training is related to a specific set of interpersonal skills (including greeting, eye contact, smiling, conversational distance, handshaking, vocal quality, small talk, polite talk) that encourage the development of behaviors that help foster good relationships with others. These skills are a must for mentors/leaders to function effectively. Using these skills, mentors/leaders should be able to adequately respond to any situation or problem. They can remain a part of the solution without exacerbating problems by an unwarranted negative shift of focus in their leadership style.

Social Skill #1--Greeting

Step One: Complete a Pre/Post Evaluation for this skill

Think of how you "come across" to others whom you know. How do they view your demeanor and attitude as they see you and interact daily with you? Think of how, without needing to compromise your basic nature and personality, you can interact positively with others through basic greetings and acknowledgment of them and their worth, and thus expand the opportunities to develop working relationships with others around you. What social skills do you need to master to accomplish your purposes?

Complete the pre-test below. The same, as a post-test, is provided in Step Seven later to use in testing what you have learned from the materials and the modeling/role play, after you have completed those exercises.

1. Define Leadership.

   _____

   _____

2. Name the three primary objectives of leadership.
   1. _____

2. _____

3. _____

3. The third leadership objective has two parts. What are they?
   1. _____
   2. _____

4. What does "effective" mean in the SEELF model?

   _____

   _____

5. What does "efficient" mean in the SEELF model

   _____

   _____

6. A mentor has three roles. What are they?
   1. _____
   2. _____
   3. _____

7. Define the term "social skills" according to the SEELF training model.

   _____

   _____

8. What are the two steps of prioritizing a goal?
   1. _____
   2. _____

9. Name six characteristics that people expect from leaders.
   1. _____

2. _____

3. _____

4. _____

5. _____

6. _____

10. What are the two types of expectations?

    1. _____

    2. _____

11. What is the second stage of learning a new skill?

_____

_____

12. What does the term *PowerGreeting* mean?

_____

_____

_____

_____

13. Successful *Power Greeting* involves these five aspects.

    1. _____

    2. _____

    3. _____

    4. _____

    5. _____

14. Role conflict is unavoidable because each person has more than one important role with many responsibilities competing for his _____, _____ and resources

15. *PowerGreeting* permits a person to make a _____ _____when meeting someone for the first time.

16. *PowerGreeting* before addressing an interpersonal conflict puts the greeter in a position to set a _____ for the discussion.

17. Every role includes three aspects leaders must consider and perfect to function effectively, including *expectations,* _____ _____*and conflict.*

18. Knowledgeable is defined as "having an experiential familiarity and understanding about the program's problems"? *(circle one)* YES or NO

19. When greeting a person it is always best to look them up and down. This "sizing them up" lets them know you are open and not intimidated. *(circle one)* YES or NO

20. Stating your accomplishments is part of the *PowerGreeting. (circle one)* YES or NO

21. Role performance is the ability to theoretically assess whether a role is being performed or not. *(circle one)* YES or NO

22. What are the five role-expectation standards?
    1. _____
    2. _____
    3. _____
    4. _____
    5. _____

23. What is the goal of *PowerGreeting?*

_____

*Step Two: Introducing **PowerGreeting with Success***

Greeting a person well is an effective skill. It is a simple way to express an important message—that the person being greeted matters, that he is important, that he has value. On a more basic level, greeting another person is an issue of respect. Failure to greet well can suggest that one considers others beneath him in some way. Such a person comes across as rude, aloof, and arrogant, and will have interpersonal problems that could be resolved by developing this simple skill.

PowerGreeting successfully involves five vital aspects:
- ✓ Conversational distance
- ✓ Establish eye contact
- ✓ Smile
- ✓ Extend handshake
- ✓ Say hello properly based on relationship and status

Step Three: Modeling the Skill/ Role Play
EXERCISE #1—The Mediator

Goal:
To learn how using *PowerGreeting* can help create a positive atmosphere between people to improve the potential for successful interpersonal communications.

Participants:
- ▪ 1 Mediator
- ▪ 2 participants

Setting:
- ▪ The mentor/leader is about to start a conflict resolution session of some type with several participants.
- ▪ The mentor/leader is seated as the group arrives for the meeting
- ▪ The mentor/leader should do the following as the group approaches:

Activity:

1. Stand up (if you are sitting)
   - Maintain proper conversational distance; at least 2-3 feet between you and the other person
     - ✓ Not too close—that says you and the person are familiar with each other
     - ✓ Not too far—that says you have some problem with the person
   - Assume a comfortable, non-confrontational stance
   - Be careful about getting too close into another's personal space
2. Look directly at a person as you greet him
   - Look calmly and non-confrontationally eye to eye
   - Keep your face level
   - Avoid roaming eyes that look the person up and down
     - ✓ Do not stare or call attention to any unusual thing about the person (appearance; hygienic problems; odd marks or features; etc.)
3. Smile
   - not too big a smile—that looks phony
   - not too little a smile—that looks disinterested
4. Form a facial expression that communicates you are peaceful, friendly, and non-judgmental
   - Guard against a look of dominance
   - Guard against a look of weakness or timidity

5. Extend a handshake
   - Firm handshake
     - ✓ Not too hard
     - ✓ Not too soft

6. Say hello

- When appropriate use each person's given name, his/her title, or nickname
- Use a greeting phrase based on proper cultural etiquette/custom
    - ✓ Formal—more reserved; no presuppositions based on race, age, etc.
    - ✓ Informal—more casual; used by those with established relationships

7. Use a direct, polite question to ask a person his name, if you do not know it:

- "You know, all this time I have seen you, I don't know your name. My name is Martin, what's your name?"

- "I don't think I have ever met you; my name is Martin, what's your name?"

EXERCISE #2—The Stranger
Goal:

To show problems that can develop when proper greeting skills are not used

Participants:
- 1 Stranger
- 1 Friend
- 4 Individuals

Setting:
- A friend approaches four acquaintances to introduce a stranger he just met
- The stranger does not use appropriate greeting skills

- When the stranger walks away the five friends talk about their first impression of the stranger

Activity:

- Do not maintain proper conversational distance with one person
- Get too close into his personal space
- Assume a somewhat confrontational stance
- Do not look directly at another as you greet him
- Look that person up and down
- Stare and call attention to any unusual thing about the person (appearance, hygienic problems; odd marks or features; etc.)
- Don't Smile
- Extend a very soft, weak handshake to another
- Say hello to only two of the four men
- Try to use a cultural greeting with another of the men as if you know the person.

Step Four: Discuss broader usages of the skill

PowerGreeting is a valuable skill for any type of interpersonal encounter whether casual or formal. A person generally feels better when he is greeted with respect. *PowerGreeting* not only makes meeting a new person easier for you and the person, but it achieves several other positive goals:

- *PowerGreeting* permits a person to make a positive first impression when meeting someone for the first time

- *PowerGreeting* before addressing an interpersonal conflict puts the greeter in a position to set a constructive atmosphere for the discussion.

- *PowerGreeting* is helpful for the greeter who needs to be accepted by opposing parties as an honest broker working in the best interest of all concerned towards a harmonious resolution of the conflict.

Step Five: Experimenting with the skill

EXERCISE #3—Practice Makes Perfect

Goal:

To give all participants an opportunity to practice the skill with various partners until each person reaches a minimum level of competency.

Participants:

Three individuals per team

- 1 Examiner role
- 1 Lead role—the person who does
- 1 Support role

Setting:

- Activities must be worked as given in the instructions without any adjustments to the role
- Workshop participants are divided into 3-man teams
- There are three role-play activities in this exercise
- The team works the same activity three times with each team member performing all three roles
- Switch partners with two other teams for the next two activities and continue the role play, until all three activities are worked with each team member playing each role

Activity # 1:

Lead role approaches both the support role and examiner role

Lead initiates all the following steps:

1. Stand up (if you are sitting)
   - Maintain proper conversational distance; at least 2-3 feet between you and the other person
     - ✓ Not too close—that says you and the person are familiar with each other
     - ✓ Not too far—that says you have some problem with the person
   - Assume a comfortable, non-confrontational stance
   - Be careful about getting too close into another personal space
2. Look directly at each person as you greet him
   - Look softly eye to eye
   - Keep your face level
   - Avoid roaming eyes that look the person up and down
     - ✓ Do not stare or call attention to any unusual thing about the person (hygienic problems; odd marks or features; etc.)
3. Smile
   - not too big a smile—that looks phony
   - not too little a smile—that looks disinterested
4. Form a facial expression that communicates you are peaceful, friendly, and non-judgmental
   - Guard against a look of dominance
   - Guard against a look of weakness
5. Extend a handshake
   - Firm handshake
     - ✓ Not too hard
     - ✓ Not too soft
6. Say hello
   - When appropriate use each person's given name, his/her title, or nickname
   - Use a greeting phrase based on proper cultural etiquette/custom

- ✓ Formal—more reserved; no presuppositions based on race, age, etc.
- ✓ Informal—more casual; used by those with established relationships

7. Use a direct, polite question to ask a person his name, if you do not know it:
   - "You know, all this time I have seen you, I don't know your name. My name is Martin, what's your name?"
   - "I don't think I have ever met you; my name is Martin, what's your name?"

Examiner observation comments

Activity # 2:
Lead role approaches both the support role and examiner role

Lead initiates all the following steps:
   - Do not maintain proper conversational distance with
   - Get too close into his personal space
   - Assume a non-confrontational stance
   - Do not look directly at another as you greet him
   - Look that person up and down
   - Stare and call attention to any unusual thing about the person (hygienic problems; odd marks or features; etc.)
   - Don't Smile
   - Extend a very soft, weak handshake to another
   - Say hello to only one of the two men (support)
   - Try to use a cultural greeting with the other man (examiner) as if you know the person

Examiner observation comments

Activity # 3 (Evaluative):

A seated Lead role player is approached by both the support role and examiner role players

Support role player initiates only the first step:

1. Support role player says, "We were sent to you because we were told you can help us"
2. Lead role player must appropriately respond according to the skills he has learned

Appropriate:

- Eye contact
- Smile
- Stand up
- Extend hand
- Handshake
- Reply

3. Support role player and examiner role player discuss the interaction as they walk away
4. Examiner observation comments

Step Six: Adapt the skill personally

Start using *PowerGreeting* and the social skills you have learned in your daily interactions with others around you. These skills can be tailored to suit who you are as a person (never phony or pretense with others) while improving your interpersonal skills substantially.

In order to personalize *PowerGreeting* one must have an understanding of how they can use the skill with their own personality. Not everyone has the same smile, hand-grip, or pleasant tone of voice. The focus should be on how we can best greet someone using the basic skills taught in the SEELF curriculum.

Avoid the tendency to do what the other person does by simply being yourself.

CRITICAL THINKING QUESTIONS:
Some personal questions to consider regarding your ability to effectively use *PowerGreeting:*
1. What part(s) of *PowerGreeting* stands out as most effective or important to you?

_____

_____

_____

2. What part(s) of *PowerGreeting* have you struggled to perform in the past?

_____

_____

_____

3. Did you struggle with any of the *PowerGreeting* steps during the activity exercises? Which ones?

_____

_____

_____

_____

4. What aspects of your personality arc the most problematic to you?

_____

_____

_____

_____

5. Do you have to adjust any of these aspects in order to effectively perform the *PowerGreeting* role?

_____

_____

_____

_____

_____

6. How will you practice *PowerGreeting* in your everyday surroundings?

_____

_____

_____

_____

_____

Step Seven: Complete the **Pre/Post Evaluation** *for this skill*

What better understanding and confidence to implement these concepts do you have now, after completing the modeling/role play exercises? Keep on "practicing" these daily until you reach that level of skills/competency where you are *consciously* skilled and *integrated* (able to perform the skill without thinking about it) as discussed in Section 5 above.

Use the following post-questions to test what you have learned and mastered as a result of the materials and modeling/role play exercises. Do not guess when answering the questions:

Do not guess when answering the questions:

1. Define Leadership.

_____

_____

2. Name the three primary objectives of leadership.
   1. _____
   2. _____
   3. _____

3. The third leadership objective has two parts. What are they?
   1. _____
   2. _____

4. What does "effective" mean in the SEELF model?

   _____

   _____

5. What does "efficient" mean in the SEELF model?

   _____

   _____

6. A mentor has three roles. What are they?
   1. _____
   2. _____
   3. _____

7. Define the term "social skills" according to the SEELF training model.

   _____

   _____

8. What are the two steps of prioritizing a goal?
   1. _____
   2. _____

9. Name six characteristics that people expect from leaders.

1. _____
2. _____
3. _____
4. _____
5. _____
6. _____

10. What are the two types of role-expectations?
    1. _____
    2. _____

11. What is the second stage of learning a new skill?

    _____

    _____

    _____

12. What does the term *PowerGreeting* mean?

    _____

    _____

13. Successful *PowerGreeting* involves these five aspects:
    1. _____
    2. _____
    3. _____
    4. _____
    5. _____

14. Role conflict is unavoidable because each person has more than one important role with many responsibilities competing for his _____, _____ and resources

15. *PowerGreeting* permits a person to make a _____ _____ when meeting someone for the first time.

16. *PowerGreeting* before addressing an interpersonal conflict puts the greeter in a position to set a _____ for the discussion.

17. Every role includes three aspects leaders must consider and perfect to function effectively, including *expectations, and conflict.*

18. Knowledgeable is defined as "having an experiential familiarity and understanding about the program's problems"? *(circle one)*
    YES   or   NO

19. When greeting a person it is always best to look them up and down. This "sizing them up" lets them know you are open and not intimidated. *(circle one)*   YES   or   NO

20. Stating your accomplishments is part of the *PowerGreeting. (circle one)*   YES   or   NO

21. Role performance is the ability to theoretically assess whether a role is being performed or not. *(circle one)*   YES   or   NO

22. What are the five role-expectation standards?
    1. _____
    2. _____
    3. _____
    4. _____
    5. _____

23. What is the goal of *PowerGreeting?*
    _____
    _____
    _____

Social Skill #2—Vocal Quality
<u>*Step One: Complete a Pre/Post Evaluation for this skill*</u>

1. Why is voice and tone an important consideration in communication skills?

_____

_____

_____

_____

_____

2. What sorts of vocal qualities do you project to others as a leader?

_____

_____

_____

3. How can *PowerGreeting* skills complement or be complemented by vocal quality and tone as you interact with others?

_____

_____

_____

_____

4. In what sorts of situations or circumstances would vocal quality and tone be especially important, and why?

_____

_____

_____

_____

Step Two: Introducing the Concept of Vocal Quality

What is your usual voice and tone? Listen to yourself and ask yourself how you "come across" to others. Are *they* likely finding your voice quality and tone to be loud, confrontational, ill-mannered, belligerent, abrasive, or disrespectful? Or do you project a voice and manner that is relaxed, calm, pleasant, agreeable, persuasive, and likely to attract and convince people rather than upsetting, angering, or offending them?

Just as important as greeting a person with proper respect, demeanor, and manner in how you stand and approach and interact with him, is to use a modulated tone and quality of voice. A person's body language "says" much, but what he *actually* says and how he says it, is just as vital to good communication skills and to maintain successful interpersonal relations.

Awareness of how we "come across" to others in our voices through modeling/role play will create the awareness of how others see us that will lead to us improving our vocal interactions.

Step Three: Modeling/Role Play

Exercise #4—VOCAL SKILLS

Goal:

To learn how to make effective use of voice skills by modeling and experimenting with different voice tones and voice projections, and making effective use of vocal components to complement the physical social greeting and engagement skills learned earlier. Vocal skills are a component and adjutant to **PowerGreeting** skills of personal presentment and demeanor.

Participants:
- 1 Mediator
- 2 Participants

Setting:

The mentor/leader informs the participant that he needs to persuade and influence the other participant in an important matter, and that he is to use his voice and tone to demonstrate his earnestness and belief on this matter to the other, and convince the other.

Activity:
- Seated facing each other.
- Maintain proper conversational distance
  - ✓ Lean forward slightly—engage the other person
  - ✓ Project earnestness and conviction
  - ✓ Look directly at the other person—convince him
- Focus on using the voice
  - ✓ To convince
  - ✓ To persuade
- Though focusing on the person directly, imagine you are speaking to him over the phone and relying on your voice alone to engage
- Next, practice the same situation, but change your voice and tone, and observe how being confrontational or strident or domineering in your tone rather than modulated, earnest and persuasive nets less-positive results or seems to fail to get your goals accomplished.

The mentor/leader informs the participant that he needs to use the earlier-learned skills of good interpersonal demeanor and engagement, but also now add the voice component in a social small talk and polite talk context. Participant in the activity is to show the other participant by use of voice and tone that he is engaging him in a non-confrontational and positive context.

Activity:

- o Standing or one participant standing approaching the seated other
  - ✓ Approach or engage in non-confrontational manner
  - ✓ Look at and directly engage the person
- o Greet the individual using voice in particular to, in turn, encourage, persuade, and convince him, but also make use of a conversational, casual small talk manner and way of doing so.

Step Four: Discuss Broader Usages of the Skill

Becoming aware of how we come across to others in our voices and tones, and then developing better vocal skills and persuasive skills, permits one to communicate with and relate to others effectively and to get things accomplished with others. A voice tone is a powerful adjutant to our actual words. The right tone gives extra strength to the words' effect upon who we are dealing with. And if we use the wrong tone, our words are robbed of their strength or effectiveness. A leader should come across to others as well-modulated, calm, and very much in-charge of the situation, rather than "throwing gasoline on the fire" or exacerbating a situation he finds himself in with others who may be emotional, irate, or unreasonable.

Step Five: Experiment with the Skill

There will invariably be many situations in a prison environment where you as a leader will need to be the well-modulated, well-toned "voice of reason" when others are "losing it" around you. Or when there are tense or confrontational situations. Do the **Critical Thinking Questions** below, discussing how vocal quality would be vital in handling the circumstances set forth in these.

CRITICAL THINKING QUESTIONS:

1. You observe a known "predator" on the unit harassing or manipulating a new young resident, while another resident stands by indifferently. What vocal qualities and tone would be essential for you to use as you address each of the three persons involved?

_____

_____

_____

2. You are approached by a highly-irate resident who is demanding something be done about some perceived injustice or wrong perpetrated against himself. What vocal qualities or tone would be essential for use to use as you address him and find out what the problem is?

_____

_____

_____

3. You are summoned to assist an aide who is being taunted or abused when he tried to quiet the dayroom. You observe many residents looking at you in a challenging, "what do you think you are you gonna do about it, huh?" fashion, while others are looking at you in a hopeful, beseeching way for you to handle it. What vocal qualities or tone would be essential to use to the aide and to each of the two groups?

_____

_____

_____

_____

_____

Step Six: Adapt the Skill Personally
Adapting the vocal quality skill will actually seem to "change your personality" to others; you will seem like "a different person", because your voice and tone will now reflect that you are a person who has self-control and quiet confidence in any interaction or situation you face. Try to practice good voice and tone in your daily life as a personal quality and expression of yourself.

Step Seven: Pre/Post-Evaluation for this skill
1. Why is voice and tone an important consideration in communication skills?

_____

_____

_____

_____

2. What sorts of vocal qualities do you project to others as a leader?

_____

_____

_____

3. How can *PowerGreeting* skills complement or be complemented by vocal quality and tone as you interact with others?

_____

_____

_____

_____

_____

_____

4. In what sorts of situations or circumstances would vocal quality and tone be especially important, and why?

_____

_____

_____

_____

_____

_____

Social Skill #3—Small Talk

Step One: Pre/Post-Evaluation for this skill
1. What is meant by "small talk?" Is small talk of small importance?

_____

_____

_____

_____

_____

_____

2. Is small talk "just passing time" or can it be an opportunity for vital interaction and achieving important purposes? How?

_____

_____

_____

_____

_____

_____

3. Why is small talk vital in leadership? How can it be used and implemented in daily leadership?

_____

_____

_____

_____

_____

_____

Step Two: Introducing the Concept of Small Talk Skill

Becoming aware of how we come across to others in our voices and tones, and then developing better vocal skills and persuasive skills, permits one to communicate with and relate to others effectively and to get things accomplished with others. Equally important in successful, everyday interpersonal relationships, however, are *small talk* skills. We are not always trying to neither convince others of something nor impart vital information; sometimes we are simply passing the time pleasantly while we wait for something or are temporarily thrown-together. Getting along agreeably with others in any context is a valuable human social skill. We want to reach a point where we have mastered this skill and have *integrated* it into our everyday life. (See Section 5, earlier in these materials).

CRITICAL THINKING QUESTIONS:

1. *You are standing "prepped" at the housing unit door with sixty other men, waiting to go to chow when the lines are run. What can you make of this opportunity to practice small talk communication skills?*

_____

_____

_____

_____

2. *You have "twenty minutes to kill" out in the housing unit dayroom while your bunkie is using the bathroom? What can you make of this opportunity to practice small talk communication skills you have learned?*

_____

_____

_____

_____

3. *You see a young participant moving onto the unit who looks lost, confused, out-of-place, or fearful? What can you make of this opportunity to practice small talk communication skills you have learned?*

_____

_____

_____

_____

_____

_____

Step Three: Modeling the Skill/Role Play
Exercise #5: Small Talking

Goal: To master simple small talk skills in a social interaction situation
Participants: A Mediator will observe as the whole group is involved.

Setting: The class group is sitting at a table, or perhaps standing around in the room.

Activity: The Mediator instructs the group that they are all together waiting for a class to begin, or at a party. The group is given ten minutes and instructed to strike up "small talk" with those around them.

They are told to try to learn something about the person next to them in a polite social context.

Evaluation: The Mediator will ask the group to give input as to how they found the "small talk" exercise to have gone? What were they able to learn about the others in this brief "small talk" context? What did he observe about those involved while they were doing the exercise?

Step Four: Discuss Broader Usages of the Skill
This course is about leadership training, ultimately. Small talk can be used in a broader, more goal-orientated context, as well, as a way to merge-into or incorporate leadership after making the other person feel comfortable with you. It is a valuable skill in order to *personalize* your leadership, to lead in a pleasant and natural seeming way, rather than in a harsh or domineering fashion. It is a valuable skill so that leaders are seen as human beings just like everyone else, and not some power elite or arrogant, standoffish sorts that no one can approach or know.

Step Five: Experiment with the Skill
Exercise 6: Small Talk Leadership/Mentoring
Goal: To successfully use small talk as an essential part of leadership/mentoring

Participants: A Mediator and two participants

Setting: The lead participant is sitting at a table, while the second person comes in, having been summoned by an aide to attend "a mentoring" from the lead due to some misconduct on his part.

Activity: The lead is instructed beforehand that he is to use "small talk" to make the to-be-mentored person feel at his ease and to develop some rapport with him before then leading smoothly and naturally into talking about the problem and mentoring him.

Evaluation: The Mediator and the rest of the class will rate how well the lead did at: putting the mentored person at ease, making the mentored person feel cared about, making the mentored person feel amenable to the purposes of their meeting, and merging naturally from small talk into the mentoring?

Step Six: Adapt the Skill Personally

By making social skills like "small talk" a natural and ordinary aspect of how you lead each day you can "lead without seeming to lead" and to be completely natural about your leadership in others' eyes. You will not seem to be aloof or apart from the people being led, but simply a leader *among* them, instead. They will feel your leadership is *personalized.* They will feel cared about.

Step Seven: Complete the Pre/Post-Evaluation

1. What is meant by "small talk?" Is small talk of small importance?

_____

_____

_____

_____

2. Is small talk "just passing time" or can it be an opportunity for vital interaction and achieving important purposes? How?

_____

_____

_____

_____

3. Why is small talk vital in leadership? How should it be used and implemented in daily leadership?

_____

_____

_____

_____

_____

Social Skill #4—Polite Talk

Step One: Complete the Pre/Post-Evaluation for this skill
a. What is polite talk? How is it different from small talk? What's the distinction?

_____

_____

_____

_____

_____

_____

b. Is polite talk always feasible in a prison environment? If you think not, why?

_____

_____

_____

c. What are the different manifestations and aspects of polite talk?

_____

_____

_____

_____

_____

Step Two: Introduce the Skill

At first blush, *small talk* and *polite talk* may perhaps seem the same to you. However, *small talk* refers more to the maintaining of a pleasant, friendly social context with others, whereas *polite talk* is far more the way and the manner in which you associate and speak with others as a polite, gentlemanly, civilized human being, period.

Polite talk is about maintaining your dignity and humanity in the midst of an undignified and inhumane environment, by learning or continuing to communicate and interact with others with civility, correctness, and courtesy, instead of with hostility, crudity, and rudeness. It is about exemplifying the time-honored concept of *being a gentleman*, about not forgetting the social graces, and about speaking and presenting yourself well, still, despite being in a place where many people feel that their surroundings justify them acting like animals.

It is about speaking and acting well as a constant example to others of how things *can* be despite where we are. It is about being a leader by example of how one *can* be civil, proper, and polite in an uncouth and rough world. Ultimately, by how *you* speak and act, you can *change* the mindset and dynamic of those around you.

Step Three: Model the Skill

All of us need to take a serious look at ourselves and how we present ourselves to other people. Do they take us seriously as a real leader and responsible, decent human being to be respected and emulated, *or* do they perceive us as a poor example, indeed, or even part of the problem? It is essential that as leaders we present ourselves as intelligent, well-spoken, well-tempered individuals, who talk-like, act-like, come-across-like someone who is worthy of respect, not as uncouth or ill-mannered individuals. Every time we speak to others, interact with others, we need to be practicing *polite talk* skills, and subtlety making a good impression upon them as to how they should be speaking, acting, and behaving toward others, their own selves.

Exercise #7: Polite Talking

Goal: To practice polite, well-spoken, civilized talk and personal presentment, and to see how *badly* the alternative can come across to others

Participants: The Mediator and two participants

Setting: Standing or sitting

Activity: The Mediator instructs the lead to first approach the other in an exaggerated style and manner practicing "prisoner" greeting, talk, and conduct ("HEEYYY! Whatz –Up, Bro!" slapping his back, executing complicated hand-clasping sequences, etc.) such as he sees others doing every day. He should strive to offend and turn-off the other individual by his too bold and familiar talk and forward, inappropriate behavior.

The non-lead will have been instructed to respond how he would if he felt offended or disrespected to be accosted or confronted by this sort of individual and talk and manner.

Then, switch partners, or have another two participants demonstrate what they believe to be a more well-mannered and well-spoken exchange, with the lead approaching the other in a respectful, courteous, and non-offensive fashion. (E.g. "Hello, my name is Martin. What's yours? I don't believe we've met before," shaking hands in proper fashion, etc.) The non-lead will have been instructed to respond how he would if he were approached instead in this polite talk and manner fashion.

CRITICAL THINKING QUESTIONS:

1. If two persons are of the same racial or cultural group, should that make a difference in what would be acceptable and polite talk in social contexts between them? Or is there some minimal standard of talk, deportment, or behavior that all of us, of whatever race or culture, ought to meet?

_____

_____

_____

all people of a certain race or culture the same in their talk and manner? Is it disrespectful or ill-advised to assume that they necessarily are?

_____

_____

_____

3. Should you lower your own personal standards of speech, deportment, and manners in order to "mentor-to" or "relate-to" an individual who is much less-sophisticated or very different than you? Is that doing your own self, and him, as well, a disservice?

_____

_____

_____

4. Should we as leaders demand a higher standard by our speech and actions from those we lead than how they happen to exemplify already?

_____

_____

_____

_____

Step Four: Discuss Broader Usages of the Skill

There is an additional concept of *polite talk* that bears discussion. *Polite talk* does not just require proper speech and manner in how we present ourselves to others, but also in what we say *about* others. Our grace and dignity as human beings not only means that we should speak well, but speak well *about* others, too. When we as leaders gossip about and talk about people to others, this is extremely disrespectful and casts us in a very bad light our own selves.

Courtesy is exemplified not only by how we are face-to-face with someone else, but also by how we do not talk bad about or slander someone who is not present. It is inappropriate and undignified for leaders to be gossips and story-spreaders about other people they are supposed to be leading and supporting. A leader who talks about others behind their backs causes people to soon no longer trust him to not also be going around talking about *them*, as well. He damages his leadership credibility. He fails to set a good example of *Higher* to those who he should be leading, by engaging in a *lower* gossiping, story-telling, betraying of trust, his own self, to anyone who will listen.

Step Five: Experiment with the Skill

Exercise #8: Hurtfulness of Impolite Talk

Goal: To teach how gossip and bad talk about others can be disrespectful, hurtful, and harmfully effect group trust

Participants: The entire group

Setting: Around the table

Activity: The Mediator hands out identical file cards to each man and instructs the men to write something bad about another man at the table. These are to be written down discreetly and immediately turned in to the Mediator. The Mediator, **without using any names**, reads aloud all the written comments.

The Mediator asks the group how they liked this activity. Many of the participants might be upset, shocked, or offended by it. Many may be feeling hurt by the comments made by others about a described person they think to be themselves. The Mediator points out to the men that this sort of thing is going on daily around the unit, and that they have surely done it themselves, and asks them how it now feels to be the butt of others' criticism? The Mediator asks the men if what they just did is becoming of a leader. He asks them to remember this activity the next time they want to talk to others in a negative way about someone.

Step Six: Adapt the Skill Personally

Polite talk is a way of speaking, behaving, and presenting ourselves well to those around us. It is what separates an articulate, responsible, to-be-respected leader and example from those around us who portray an uncouth talk and manner and who are not yet ready for leadership and have much personal growth and maturity and sophistication to still accomplish. It is an important social skill to truly *integrate* into your personal leadership repertoire.

Step Seven: Pre/Post-Evaluation

1. What is polite talk? How is it different from small talk? What's the distinction?

   _____

   _____

   _____

   _____

2. Is polite talk always feasible in a prison environment? If you think not, why?

_____

_____

_____

_____

_____

3. What are the different manifestations and aspects of polite talk?

_____

_____

_____

_____

COMMUNICATION SKILLS

Step One: Complete the Pre/Post-Evaluation

1. What are some ways (mannerisms, body language, etc.) that we communicate with others besides the spoken word?

_____

_____

_____

_____

2. How does one listen in search of meaning versus listening defensively to find fault, loopholes, or weaknesses in the thoughts of others?

_____

_____

_____

_____

3. Define the five types of listening/communication: reflective, empathetic, thoughtful, plain talk, and body talk:

_____

_____

_____

_____

_____

4. What type of listening/communication (see Question 3, above) would be most useful in each of the following contexts? Trying to understand the feelings of a resident who has just lost a loved one.

5. Telling someone a truth about themselves
Gauging someone's demeanor/mannerisms to be different than their words. Helping a young foolish resident to see how his conduct looks to others. When someone says "Can you 'feel' me?"

Step Two: Introduce the Skill

Effective communication skills are foundational to successful relationships. No aspect of interaction between people is of greater significance than communication. It requires constant sharpening of the tools we use to listen for intent/feeling as others speak to us and to speak to others in a way that expresses our thoughts and feelings clearly.

Communication incorporates our being able to carry out various roles or objectives in different contexts to suit that particular situation. Some of the different sorts of listening/communication are set forth in greater detail below.

Of equal importance is how we present ourselves during conversations; our facial expression, the way we stand, what we do with our hands, the look of our eyes. Body language tells its own tale and can determine how well our words are accepted by others.

Training to be a more effective communicator is especially vital for being a good mentor. Very few people receive adequate training for normal communication. How does one listen in search of meaning versus listening defensively to find fault, loopholes, or weaknesses in the thoughts of others? What is the best way to express one's thoughts and feelings clearly without being too vulnerable but to properly communicate one's true intention? How can we be sure others are understanding us clearly, and how can we be sure we are understanding them clearly?

Step Three: Modeling the Skill
Good communication is all about modeling your listening/communication style to the situation at-hand, and making use of the appropriate concepts to best lead and facilitate the person you are speaking-with or mentoring.

Some effective listening/communication concepts to know about, include:
1. Reflective listening
2. Empathetic listening
3. Thoughtful listening
4. Plain talk
5. Body talk

In *Step Four*, below, these broader usages of listening/communication are discussed in greater detail. Read ahead briefly to familiarize yourself with these models before doing the modeling/role play exercises further along.

Exercise #9: Modeling Listening Skills

Goal: To practice and model the three types of listening skills
Participants: The Mediator and two different participants for each skill to be modeled

Setting: The two participants sit across from one another, preferably with no table or barrier between themselves

Activity: The Mediator advises the participants that they are to practice, in turn, the concepts of reflective listening, empathetic listening, and thoughtful listening.

For reflective listening skills practice, one of the participants might be griping about the mentoring program's rules or procedures, while the other in turn shows him how he is appearing to others and the fallacy of his reasoning and methods.

For empathetic listening skills practice, one of the participants might be telling the other about problems at home or his struggles in the program, while the other shows empathy and care.

For thoughtful listening skills practice, one of the participants might be subtly or obliquely asking for sympathy, advice, help, or support in some way, while the other needs to listen thoughtfully and discern what the other is *really* meaning or trying to say.

Exercise #10: Modeling Plain Talk and Body Talk Skills

Goal: To practice and model the plain talk and body talk types of listening skills

Participants: The Mediator and two different participants for each skill to be modeled

Setting: The two participants sit across from one another, preferably with no table or barrier between themselves

Activity: The Mediator advises the participants that they are to practice, in turn, the concepts of plain talk and body talk. In the latter modeling exercise, the group should be asked what body talk it specifically observed the lead and the other involved person to be manifesting as the interaction occurred.

Step Four: Discuss Broader Usages of the Skill
There are always different types or models of communication being used by us in our interactions with others, often unconsciously.

In ***reflective listening***, the listener seeks to be "a mirror" of the speaker, "reflecting" back to him in an engaged, positive way what he is saying, and helping him to feel affirmed and "heard." The listener, also, by acting as "a mirror" can help the speaker to his own self to "see himself" and his own self become aware of what he is saying, how he is appearing, and any fallacies or flaws in his own thinking, without the listener seeming to be judgmental, critical, or uncaring. Communication is a two-way street, and two-way-exchange, between two people. Each person engaged in their conversation or interaction is giving back and forth between themselves and the other constantly as they go along.

Empathetic listening is when a listener seeks to place himself in the same shoes as the speaker, and to "feel" himself what the speaker is saying and wishing to impart or get-across. (Hence, the expression, "Can you 'feel' me?") He is seeking to empathize with "where the speaker is coming from." He wants to understand why the speaker feels as he does. And he wants to let the speaker know that he cares enough to want to understand how the speaker feels.

Thoughtful listening is when the listener is weighing or testing the speaker's words and thoughts in his own mind. He is seeking not just to understand what the speaker is wishing to impart or get-across, but also what it *means*, and even what the speaker *really means*. What is really behind what the speaker is saying or feeling? What can the listener discern about where the speaker is coming-from, needing, or seeking? It is going beneath the surface words to really ascertain what the speaker is trying to deeply but emphatically communicate.

Plain talk refers to expressing one's self through words in an open, honest, and forthright fashion to another human being. It is plainly meaning what you plainly state. It is unembellished, from the heart and mind, communication and interaction. *Body talk* is getting across your message or how you are feeling by the unspoken body language and mannerisms we all do almost unconsciously. Both *plain* talk and *body talk* are both going on at the same time during any conversation and communication. Actual words are being spoken, but unspoken body language is also occurring. One should always be conscious of both and how both are part of the process of communication and interaction. Sometimes the words do not match the body language at all. Think back to the practical exercises and role-plays that you did earlier in this training course, and how body language and tone often influenced drastically how you reacted to what the other participant was saying during those.

CRITICAL THINKING QUESTIONS:

1. *Write a short example of when you might make practical use of reflective, empathetic, or thoughtful listening in a common daily situation.*

_____

_____

_____

_____

2. *Write a short example of a situation you have been in where a person's body language and plain talk were contrary to each other?*

_____

_____

_____

_____

_____

3. *Can someone be an effective leader or mentor without good communications skills? Why or why not?*

_____

_____

_____

_____

4. *Have you ever had an inability to understand or communicate-with* AT ALL *another individual? What was causing the problem, do you think? How might the impasse or inability have been overcome?*

_____

_____

_____

Step Five: Experiment with the Skill

We often already do unconsciously the skills of reflective, empathetic, and thoughtful thinking, and plain talk and body talk, in our everyday conversations and interactions. But to be more effective leaders, we need to consciously select when necessary the right type of listening to engage in, based upon each new situation we are confronted-with, and consciously-apply it. Try through experimentation and practice to realize what each person's situation or mindset calls for from you, and "deliver" that for them. A common failure in communication, in fact, is when we don't understand what a person "is really saying" or "really needing", right then, as they speak to us. We must as leaders strive to "dig deeper" to communicate, relate, and lead better.

Step Six: Adapt the Skill Personally

Some men are better at certain communication skills than others. Some men have people come to them because they are "a good listener", that is, empathetic; or are perceived as "wise", that is, thoughtful or discerning in their listening and response; or are excellent at helping others find their own answers, that is, good reflective listeners. Whatever your particular gift or strength is, use that as a leader to do good where you can. There is a need for leaders and leadership of every sort and variety. You never need to be "fake" or "pretentious" toward others. Just be yourself, and you will do well in whatever ways you are best at.

Step Seven: Pre/Post-Evaluation

1. What are some ways (mannerisms, body language, etc.) that we communicate with others besides the spoken word?

_____

_____

_____

2. How does one listen in search of meaning versus listening defensively to find fault, loopholes, or weaknesses in the thoughts of others?

_____

_____

_____

3. empathetic, thoughtful, plain talk, and body talk:

_____

_____

_____

_____

4. What type of listening/communication (see Question 3, above) would be most useful in each of the following contexts?

Trying to understand the feelings of a resident who has just lost a loved one.
Telling someone a truth about themselves. Gauging someone's demeanor/mannerisms to be different than their words
Helping a young foolish resident to see how his conduct looks to others
When someone says "Can you 'feel' me?"

CONFRONTATIONAL SKILLS

Step One: Complete the Pre/Post-Evaluation

1.   *What sort of problems does a leader typically have to confront and deal with in managing a group dynamic? What difficulties are inherent in any group situation? What "traits" does such a successful group exemplify?*

_____

_____

_____

2.   *What are the key factors that influence the ability of individuals and groups to interact well?*

_____

_____

_____

_____

_____

3.   *Describe some of the techniques a leader can use to bring harmony and good function to a group dynamic to achieve its purposes and goals.*

_____

_____

_____

Step Two: Introduce the Skill

A leader must be able to confront and deal-with the problems inherent in managing a group and in handling the differing personalities, psyches, egos, necessarily "at war" within that dynamic. *Confrontational skills* do not refer to angry interpersonal confrontation, but rather to confronting normal human relations problems and overcoming them. Confrontation skills are important for managing small group discussions and helping to resolve interpersonal conflicts. A mentor works to cultivate within groups those qualities that promote program goals, including trust, acceptance, freedom of self-expression, and the ability to relax together and share thoughts and feelings openly.

Several key factors influence the ability of individuals and groups to interact well:

1. Personality and style of the leaders
2. The degree of commonality shared by group members
3. The degree to which a group shares expectations and commitments equally
4. Avoiding patterns of interaction that tend to create a defensive group climate:
    a. Evaluations vs. descriptions
    b. Manipulation vs. motivation

5. Identifying disharmony
6. Identifying conflict
7. Identifying discrepancies
8. Distinguishing between the natural discomfort people feel when interacting on more than a surface level (primary tension), and personality conflicts (secondary tension)
9. Identifying mixed messages in:
    a. Thought
    b. Behavior
    c. Feelings
    d. Meaning

CRITICAL THINKING QUESTIONS:

1. *What skills does an effective group leader need to have?*

_____

_____

_____

2. *What makes for a harmonious group versus a disharmonious group? How can you tell if a group is disharmonious or at odds?*

_____

_____

_____

3. *Can a group that is not essentially harmonious still accomplish its goals and purposes successfully by shared commitment, goal, and purposes? Or does group efficacy necessarily require getting along?*

_____

_____

_____

4. *Is it better for a group to have variety, or commonality? To have many opinions, or consensus? To agree, or respectfully disagree? Why? How might a leader still make internal group disharmony a plus?*

_____

_____

_____

_____

Step Three: Model the Skill
Exercise #11: Patterns of Interaction
Goal: Avoiding patterns of interaction that tend to create a defensive group climate:
- o Evaluations vs. descriptions
- o Manipulation vs. motivation

Participants: The Mediator, two participants, and the group
Setting: A "leader" role-play speaking to a group
Activity: The "leader" is instructed to first describe some of the group's members and their talents and abilities in a blunt, critical, very evaluative

fashion. Next, he is then instructed to show the difference, by describing some of the group's members and their talents and abilities in a still honest fashion, but avoiding seeming to evaluate them critically.

Another "leader" then is instructed to first pretend to be addressing the group in a highly-manipulative fashion to "force" them to agree with him or do things his way. Next, he is then instructed to instead, to show the difference, pretend to be addressing the group in a highly-motivational fashion in an effort to accomplish the same goals he had earlier, now in a way that induces the group's willing cooperation and enthusiasm to fulfill those goals.

Exercise #12: Identifying Problems Within the Group
Goal:

Identifying disharmony

Identifying conflict

Identifying discrepancies

Distinguishing between the natural discomfort people feel when interacting on more than a surface level (primary tension), and personality conflicts (secondary tension)

Identifying mixed messages in:
- Thought
- Behavior
- Feelings
- Meaning

Participants: Seven pre-selected members of the group

Setting: The meeting room table

Activity: Before the group meets, unbeknownst to anyone else, the Mediator speaks to seven different members of the group, each of them separately, and separately, unbeknownst to one another, asks each of them to deliberately try to disrupt and frustrate the purposes of the group.

He tells one participant to arrive late for the group in a loud, boisterous, rude fashion, totally interrupting the proceedings.

He tells a second participant who will be already there to constantly be combative, smart-mouthed, snide, rude, and interrupting as the group tries to meet and carry out its purposes.

He tells a third participant to act as a "know-it-all", interjecting his opinions on every point, interrupting anyone who speaks, and demanding to get his own way and preference in every respect, whatever is being said or done.

He tells a fourth participant to be complaining and unhappy all through the group meeting, and generally making everyone else around him miserable with his malcontent and whining.

He tells a fifth participant to sit in stony silence with his arms folded, scowling, defiant in manner, refusing to participate in any fashion, and ignoring even the group leader no matter what he is asked to do or contribute.

He tells a sixth and seventh participant to come in and act all through the group as though they are quarreling and angry with one another over some outside matter going on between them. They are to "bring their business" with them into the group, continuing to argue and bicker over something that no one else in the group knows anything about.

After the group has, predictably, descended into total chaos and stalemate, with nothing going forward or being achieved, the Mediator will explain to the participants what the exercise has been about, and ask the group to identify and categorize the group-destructive behaviors each of the participants was exemplifying. The Mediator will explain how bad behaviors and everyone in total conflict in a group can be destroy group efficacy or productiveness. And he will emphasize to them how a leader will inevitably have at least "one of each of these sorts" of persons in almost any group he is leading or mentoring, and that to be an effective leader he must learn to deal with such challenges to the group's success.

Step Four: Discuss Broader Usages of the Skill

Confrontational skills of a leader are important to "keep order" and "do traffic control" when dealing with another person or a group who is off-point or in discord as to what the priority right then needs to be. A group leader needs to be able to firmly take charge in getting a person in it or the group as a whole "back in line" and "back on focus." As demonstrated by Exercise #12 above, a group or objective can all too-easily be sidetracked totally by persons who are not cooperating, who are being disruptive, or who are bringing their own side-issues, personal agendas, or self-interests into the proceedings. An effective, skillful leader knows how to "confront" these persons in a manner that does not alienate them but directs them clearly and firmly back to what is trying to be accomplished and the correct focus of everyone needed to achieve it.

Step Five: Experiment with the Skill

As a follow-up to Exercise #12 above, the men in the group or class should discuss how they could, as a leader, have dealt with each of the different "types" of problems presented by the acting-up men in it. What is the best approach to use as a leader in handling interpersonal or group waywardness? Does each different "type" of problem require different techniques to deal-with-it? Experiment with what a leader can do to focus his group and "keep order" in it.

Step Six: Adapt the Skill Personally

All persons, all leaders, bring different personalities, natures, and skills and talents to the leadership process. What "works" for one leader, may be impossible or ineffective or even seem false or contrived, when tried by another. Ultimately, being one's self even while definitely still being a leader, will get the job done best. There are no right or wrong ways to be yourself, so long as they accomplish your goal of leadership, and do seem to others to be leadership. (This does not mean that a leader should "lower himself" to the level of those he deals with, nor that he should try to act like them to interact successfully with them. A leader should always still, for example, practice *polite talk*, be a gentleman, present himself as a responsible and articulate individual to be taken seriously, no matter what.)

Step Seven: Complete the Pre/Post-Evaluation

1. *What sort of problems does a leader typically have to confront and deal with in managing a group dynamic? What difficulties are inherent in any group situation?*

_____

_____

_____

_____

_____

2. *What "traits" does such a successful group exemplify?*

_____

_____

_____

_____

_____

3. *What are the key factors that influence the ability of individuals and groups to interact well?*

_____

_____

_____

_____

4. *Describe some of the techniques a leader can use to bring harmony and good function to a group dynamic to achieve its purposes and goals.*

_____

_____

_____

_____

FACILITATING SKILLS

Step One: Complete the Pre/Post-Evaluation

1. How do *you* define a "facilitator"? What skills and talents should such a person have?

_____

_____

_____

_____

2. What are some of the reasons that a facilitator might prove indispensable, even amidst capable leaders?

_____

_____

_____

_____

3. What social and communications skills that have been studied earlier in this course would a facilitator need to use or employ?

_____

_____

_____

_____

_____

_____

_____

Step Two: Introducing the Skill

Recall the definition for "facilitator" that was given at the start of this course. A facilitator is defined as "one who helps to bring about an outcome (as learning, productivity, or communication) by providing indirect or unobtrusive assistance, guidance, or supervision."

A skilled facilitator combines and incorporates all the communication skills to accomplish effective leadership in an interpersonal or group leadership dynamic "without seeming to." The special gift of the facilitator is that his is unobtrusive and subtle leadership. He helps others come to a harmonious and workable solution among themselves without imposing his leadership authority, per se.

Everyone, even leaders, could use someone, sometime, to guide and assist or focus them. In a group dynamic, even a group of leaders, disparate or disharmonious persons can be brought together enough to at least work together, by an intuitive and trained facilitator. *Confrontational skills* set out in Section D above, well-employed by a skillful facilitator, can overcome group dysfunctions and tensions and disharmony in order to "get the job done" as a group working effectively together for common goals and purposes.

167

Step Three: Modeling the Skill
EXERCISE # 13: FACILITATION

GOAL: To learn simple facilitation skills

PARTICIPANTS: One participant is assigned to be "a facilitator" for three other men in the group. There can be several such groups of four.

ACTIVITY: Each "facilitator" is to present a problem or issue involving the program to his group of three other men (e.g. too much noise in the dayroom, a dispute involving the aides, dissatisfaction with how things are being done, etc.), and then mediate and facilitate them as they present ideas and opinions upon that topic. He is to help them arrive at a leadership solution to that problem or issue, BUT to have, in the correct sense and spirit of facilitation, made it seem to them that they solved the problem or disagreement themselves, without him "imposing" it upon them or "telling them what to do."

CRITICAL THINKING QUESTIONS:

1. *Discuss the concept of facilitation group leadership and what it means, as opposed to individual leadership?*

_____

_____

_____

_____

2. *What confrontational skills should a group leader use to combat problems like complete disagreement within the group?*

_____

_____

_____

_____

_____

3. *What confrontational skills should a facilitator or group leader use to combat problems like clashing egos or personalities in his group?*

_____

_____

_____

_____

_____

4. *Should leaders accept facilitation/leadership in order to lead? Discuss this idea.*

_____

_____

_____

_____

_____

_____

Step Four: Discuss Broader Usages of the Skill

A facilitator can be called and considered many things: a leader, a group leader, a mediator, a mentor, an advisor, a muse. He is functioning in whatever regard the persons involved and the situation may require. He is "wearing many hats," yet his role of assisting and helping remains the same, in whatever capacity he is operating just then.

Step Five: Experiment with the Skill

The facilitator does not need a formal title or job function as such, in order to facilitate. Every day a leader will be called on or needed to mediate and facilitate in interactions very informally and spontaneously, as he interacts-with and deals with other people just in general. Indeed, by definition, a facilitator is a person who brings about an outcome without seeming to be a leader dictating the result or telling others what to do. A facilitator is "the leader who leads least" while mentoring and encouraging others to step up and solve their difficulties or find solutions themselves.

As he embraces his facilitation role and his skill grows, he will find himself naturally and automatically and smoothly "functioning as a facilitator" around others. A facilitator is a "smooth operator." He encourages, he guides, he motivates, instead of directing, demanding, or setting forth ultimatums. But he is one of the most effective individuals in the program.

Step Six: Adapt the Skill Personally

There are all sorts of facilitators and facilitations. There are some individuals who will be able to lead and facilitate and mentor with credibility and effectiveness in some segments of the program's residents that others would not be able to in the same way. The program specifically recognizes this truth. However, a capable facilitator should still be able to function amidst any group or dynamic in his surroundings by simply guiding the persons in finding solutions in their own ways, rather than trying to impose his beliefs or opinions upon them. But he also holds them to the standard of them needing to find a way and to show some results. He does NOT just simply excuse them or exempt them from acting right and achieving what needs accomplished or improved. A facilitator helps people help themselves, but also looks to them to get the job done.

Step Seven: Complete the Pre/Post-Evaluation

1. How do *you* define a "facilitator"? What skills and talents should such a person have?

_____

_____

_____

_____

2. What are some of the reasons that a facilitator might prove indispensable, even amidst capable leaders?

_____

_____

_____

_____

3. What social and communications skills that have been studied earlier in this course would a facilitator need to use or employ?

_____

_____

_____

_____

_____

COPING SKILLS

Step One: Complete the Pre/Post-Evaluation

1. List three things that indicate when a leader/mentor may be showing signs that he is overloaded and under stress.

_____

_____

_____

_____

_____

2. List three things that a leader/mentor can do to cope and manage when he is overloaded and under stress.

_____

_____

_____

_____

Step Two: Introduce the Skill

A facilitator, a mentor, a leader, is only human. He may be trapped in the midst of the same circumstances and situations as everyone else around him. He may struggle with personal difficulties and stress his own self on a daily basis. He may become overworked, overwhelmed, and exhausted in his duties and functions. (The exhaustion may be emotional as well as physical.) He may become the focal point of criticism from others or be unable to please everyone, or even be caught in the middle between warring factions. Ultimately, he may need to become aware of his own situation and self-limitations and seek help and assistance his own self before he can help others effectively with their struggles or disharmony. Awareness of the situation he finds himself in, will be the starting point for him to then proceed to develop needed *coping skills.*

Step Three: Modeling the Skill
Exercise #14: Recognizing Leadership Stress

Goal: To learn to recognize symptoms of stress in a leader or mentor

Participants: The class divides up into pairs

Setting: Seated face to face in chairs, or across the table from one another

Activity: Each person in the pair will question the other in a friendly, conversational fashion about how he is doing in his present job, duties, or leadership or mentoring role. They will seek to sense or ascertain if the other person may be showing some signs of overwork, stress, tension, or inability to cope-with, his tasks or load.

Step Four: Discuss Broader Usages of the Skill
Coping skills for a facilitator, mentor, or leader, include the following:

1. Noticing and properly interpreting the seriousness of the toll emotions and personal issues can take upon him
2. Realizing how these may be affecting his judgment and reasoning abilities, or may be obscuring things he should be noticing or realizing about others
3. Seeking assistance from others when the workload becomes too great and delegating
4. Seeking help and wise counsel his own self when he is himself struggling with emotions or difficulties beyond his self-management
5. Adhering to the advice of others when his own judgment is impaired
6. Developing a plan to manage his time and emotions so that he can continue to function in his capacities to manage and assist others. Following through on and sticking with that plan.

CRITICAL THINKING QUESTIONS:

1. Do you believe that some people are excellent at leading or managing others, but fail to lead or manage their own selves? Assess if they can and should be leading?

_____

_____

_____

_____

2. How should a leader go about delegating part of his tasks to others in order to cope? What degree of responsibility does he still retain over those delegated tasks?

_____

_____

_____

_____

_____

3. Can a leader decide that the advice of others about himself and his leadership should be disregarded? In what situations? When? Why?

_____

_____

_____

_____

_____

_____

_____

_____

Step Five: Experiment with the Skill

Practice the skill of identifying problems a leader/mentor may be having and assisting him in coping with those, by doing the exercise below:

EXERCISE #15: HELPING THE STRUGGLING LEADER

GOAL: To find remedies and solutions to assist the overworked, stressed, or struggling leader/mentor

PARTICIPANTS: The group as a whole

SETTING: Around the table as a discussion group

ACTIVITY: After having completed Exercise #13 above, the group as a whole will meet to try to offer suggestions and solutions to the identified stressors or problems that came to light during the previous pairs' discussions. They will function to assist by offering ways that the leaders/mentors can deal with their stresses, problems, and struggles in leadership and mentoring, and in the process learn the skill of *coping*.

Step Six: Adapt the Skill Personally

Each leader and mentor needs to frankly look at themselves and see how well they are *coping*.

No leader is immune from the problems of overwork, stress, and struggle. Every leader is human and fallible, and has limits and breaking points. Leaders help other leaders with *coping*, as they also listen to others who can give them insights into how they themselves can better *cope*.

Step Seven: Complete the Pre/Post-Evaluation
1. List three things that indicate when a leader/mentor may be showing signs that he is overloaded and under stress.

_____

_____

_____

_____

_____

2. List three things that a leader/mentor can do to cope and manage when he is overloaded and under stress.

_____

_____

_____

_____

_____

INFLUENCING SKILLS

Step One: Complete the Pre/Post-Evaluation
1. Define the three primary leadership roles in the leadership model.

_____

_____

_____

_____

2. Define each of the different roles of influence of the Mentor:
Friend

_____

Tutor

_____

Coach

_____

3. What is the difference between a teacher and a facilitator?

_____

_____

_____

_____

_____

_____

4. What are the *Five Expectation* Standards required for any leadership role?

_____

_____

_____

_____

5. What are the six personal qualities or traits that people expect of leaders?

_____

_____

_____

_____

Step Two: Introducing the Skill

There is an important expression that all leaders, mentors, and facilitators should never forget. It states: "When you gain power, use it wisely and well." If you have gained power, don't misuse it or abuse it. Be worthy of it. Keep the trust of those whom you lead. Keep the respect of those whom you govern. Remember that you have, in the eyes of those who you are leading, mentoring, and facilitating, credibility and integrity, but only so long as you continue to earn it.

Always remember, too, that, along with power, you now have *Influence*. You can influence by words, but you also influence by actions and your demonstrated personal integrity. You have the ability to use your influence for the good of the group, or misuse it. The choice is yours, and it is the ultimate decision you will have to make as a leader.

Step Three: Modeling the Skill
Exercise #16: Defining Peer-Leadership

Goal: To model and identify different types of peer-leadership
Participants: Five participants, who each in turn, will model or role-play a particular peer-leadership role
Setting: Addressing the group, standing at head of table

Activity: Each of the five participants, in turn, will demonstrate the different types of peer-group leadership, by role-playing 1) a friend, 2) a tutor, 3) a coach, 4) a facilitator, and 5) a teacher. Each is to portray each of these roles in the manner in which he feels a person would present themselves, speak, or address the group, if fulfilling these particular leadership functions to them. The group seeks, after each, to identify the peer-group leadership role that has been demonstrated, and discusses how that particular role was effective in getting group-leadership purposes accomplished.

Step Four: Discuss Broader Usages of the Skill

This is a good time to go back to the start of this Guide and review again the roles of a leader discussed and defined immediately following the Introduction.

Recall from the Introduction, that definitions of leadership and leadership skills can either be theoretical or practical. Theoretical definitions usually offer a general viewpoint of a word, relying on abstract principles and speculation. Practical definitions give information that goes beyond theory or ideal; it is useful information that is action oriented and capable of being put to use. Practical definitions were used throughout this series to highlight the action associated with the terms defined, especially helpful when discussing leadership roles. The definition of the terms discloses the action associated with the leadership role.

Leader—one whose ideas, strength, and courageous acts guide others on the way and directs their behavior in a manner that causes them to follow.

Leadership—influence of a group of leaders who work in concert with each other to initiate and activate change and direct the movement of their group towards clearly defined goals. Three primary leadership objectives:
>   1. How to delegate
>   2. How to motivate
>
>   3. How to regulate
>   One's self
>   Others

Effective—having and using the ability and power to accomplish actual purpose and intent.

Efficient—properly and adequately using all available resources in the most useful and least wasteful manner possible to achieve an intended purpose.

Notice that a leader uses effective and efficient methods to *influence* a group to work in concert with each other to initiate and activate change and to move toward clearly defined goals. Leadership is synonymous with *influence*, which, in fact, is a core value and concept of mentoring. A leader *influences* be delegating, motivating, regulating, others.

Step Five: Experiment with the Skill
Leadership role-performance is related to how a role is *actually* being performed (despite how it should be performed), which may or may not align with either a person's self-imposed expectations or the expectations others have of him.

Performance objectives should include—specific information defining the role from broad perspectives including:

What the role involves (specific duties, scheduling issues, reports, personal sacrifices, etc.)
    Timelines
    Performance measures and methods
Evaluation of one's personal ability to perform:
    How to get the most out of one's strengths?
    How to improve one's weaknesses?
    How to determine the limits of one's ability?

As one begins to experiment-with and use his new leadership parameters, he must constantly be setting performance objectives for himself, developing how he will fulfill those objectives, and then assessing how he has done in carrying out those objectives. He must determine how he can best be a leader by knowing himself and how he best functions and what personal obstacles he needs to overcome or what reorganization of his habits might be necessary, for him to effectively fulfill his leadership goals and objectives. How well he does in managing *himself* will show clearly to others how good he is as a leader. He will best *influence* others by the example of himself.

Step Six: Develop the Skill Personally

Finally, from the <u>Introduction</u> of this guide, that leadership role is all about *expectations.*

<u>Type One Expectations—What do you expect of yourself?</u>
Measure each item your personal self-expectations as a leader list by the *Five Expectation Standards* list. Determine if each expectation you list is:

Reasonable, Just, Proper, Due and Necessary

Also, consider and examine expectations that other people have of you as a leader.

<u>Type Two Expectations—What do people expect of leaders?</u> A leader is expected by others to have:
1. **Integrity** (be honest, sound and principled (incorruptible))
2. **Trustworthiness** (be worthy of confidence; dependable)
3. **Respectfulness** (considerate, consider others worthy of high regard)
4. **Loyalty** (be unswerving allegiance to others; faithful to the cause, ideal, custom)
5. **Activeness** (be fully engaged, energetic and action-oriented)
6. **Knowledge** (experiential familiarity and understanding & solutions to problems)

There is an old saying, "Physician, heal thyself." A leader has to first put his own house in order before he presumes to go clean up other men's houses. A leader needs to *know himself* and *regulate himself*. Functioning effectively in any peer leadership role requires "personal inventory" to call attention to any personal attitude, belief, practice, or position one may have that could negatively impact one's ability to lead another. So that he can lead, and be a good leader, a leader embarking upon leadership should initially examine his own:

Personal Awareness
Predispositions—values/beliefs one has that affect the way he receives, accepts, interacts, or relates with another

Assumptions—one's supposition that something is true, factual and is likely taken for granted

Perceptions—a formed mental position/image interpreted in light of one's collective personal experiences

Personal Disciplines
Modeling the change one want others to adopt
Exemplifying self-control and self-discipline
Maintaining positive lifestyle and good personal conduct

The would-be leader also needs to honestly assess how he personally "handles" power and influence. He needs to be aware of the dynamics of power positions:

Power Positions
Privileges of the position

Challenges of the position

Responsibilities of the position

How will one deal with the privileges, challenges, and responsibilities of his new-found responsibilities and influences? Will he rise above his own human frailties and faults? Will he be able to resist misusing his authority and power? Will he exhibit the personal self-awareness and personal discipline to be a true leader among men? These are the ultimate and greatest challenges of leadership.

How do *you,* the would-be leader, stack up? How will *you* be and do as a leader? Can you cut-it as a leader? Are you willing to do the work, and to try? Only you yourself know the answers to these questions; only you can find out the answers to these questions. The task is at hand.

Step Seven: Complete the Pre/Post-Evaluation
1. Define the three primary leadership roles in the leadership model.

_____

_____

_____

2. Define each of the different roles of influence of the Mentor:

Friend _____

Tutor _____

Coach _____

3. What is the difference between a teacher and a facilitator?

_____

_____

_____

_____

4. What are the *Five Expectation* Standards required for any leadership role?

_____
_____
_____
_____

5. What are the six personal qualities or traits that people expect of leaders?

_____
_____
_____
_____
_____
_____
_____
_____
_____
_____

CRITICAL THINKING QUESTIONS:

What have you learned about leadership in this training course? What was very useful about the course and what was less useful? Are you prepared to do the personal work needed and show the necessary integrity, to become an influential leader? ARE YOU A LEADER?

_____
_____
_____
_____
_____
_____
_____

_____
_____
_____
_____
_____
_____
_____
_____
_____
_____
_____
_____
_____
_____
_____
_____
_____
_____
_____
_____
_____
_____
_____

To contact Martin E. Thomas for Workshop Facilitation, Keynote Speaking, Conference participation and other book related experiences:

MET@fsfg.org
www.fsfg.org

On the Road to Manhood

CPSIA information can be obtained
at www.ICGtesting.com
Printed in the USA
FSHW021010160419
57302FS